MENSA
PUZZLE
CHALLENGE
3

Also available in the Mensa series
If you've enjoyed Mensa Puzzle Challenge, why not take a look at some of the other books in the ground-breaking Mensa series.

Mensa Ultimate Puzzle Challenge
By Philip Carter, Ken Russell & John Bremner
ISBN 1 85868 716 0 (304 pages).

Mensa Mighty Mind Maze
By John Bremner
ISBN 1 85868 649 0 (224 pages).

Mensa Covert Challenge
By David Colton
ISBN 1 85868 745 4 (224 pages).

Mensa Mind Assault Course
By Dave Chatten & Carolyn Skitt
ISBN 1 85868 467 6 (224 pages).

Mensa Challenge Your IQ
By Philip Carter, Ken Russell & John Bremner
ISBN 1 85868 473 0 (224 pages).

Mensa Compendium of Conundrums
By Peter Jackson
ISBN 1 85868 457 9 (224 pages).

Mensa Crosswords
By Peter Jackson & Ken Russell
ISBN 1 85868 447 1 (224 pages).

Mensa Lateral Thinking & Logical Deduction
By Dave Chatten & Carolyn Skitt
ISBN 1 85868 472 2 (224 pages).

Mensa Assess Your Personality
By Robert Allen
ISBN 1 85868 468 4 (224 pages).

Mensa Puzzle Challenge
By Robert Allen
ISBN 1 85868 933 3 (256 pages).

Mensa Puzzle Challenge 2
By Robert Allen
ISBN 1 85868 954 6 (256 pages).

These Mensa books and many others are available from all good bookshops, or they may be ordered by telephone in the UK from Bookpost on (01624) 836 000.

THIS IS A CARLTON BOOK

Text and puzzle content copyright © British Mensa Limited 2001
Design and artwork copyright © Carlton Books Limited 2001

This edition published by Carlton Books Limited in 2001

A CIP catalogue record for this book is available from the British Library

UK ISBN 1 84222 230 9
US ISBN 1 84222 399 2

Project Editors: Lara Maiklem, Kerrin Edwards
Art Director: Mark Lloyd
Puzzle Checking: John Paines
Original Puzzles Created by: Robert Allen, Carolyn Skitt

Printed in Dubai

MENSA
PUZZLE
CHALLENGE
3

Robert Allen

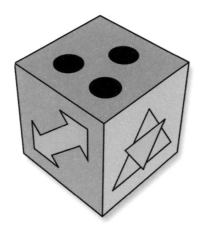

CARLTON
BOOKS

British Mensa Limited

British Mensa Limited is an organization for individuals who have one common trait: an IQ in the top two per cent of the nation. Over 30,000 current members have found out how bright they are. This leaves room for over a million members in Britain alone. You may be one of them.

Looking for mental stimulation?

If you enjoy mental exercise, you'll find lots of good "workout programmes" in our national monthly magazine. Voice your opinion in one of the newsletters published by our many local chapters. Learn from the many books and publications that are available to you as a member.

Looking for social interaction?

Are you a "people person", or would you like to meet other people with whom you feel comfortable? Then come to our local meetings, parties and get-togethers. Participate in our lectures and debates. Attend our regional events and national gatherings. There's something happening on the Mensa calendar almost daily. So, you have lots of opportunities to meet people, exchange ideas and make interesting new friends.

Looking for others who share your special interest?

Whether yours is as common as crossword puzzles or as esoteric as Egyptology, there's a Mensa Special Interest Group (SIG) for it.

Take the challenge. Find out how smart you really are. Contact British Mensa Ltd today and ask for a free brochure. We enjoy adding new members and ideas to our high-IQ organization.

British Mensa Ltd
St John's House
St John's Square
Wolverhampton WV2 4AH

Or, if you don't live in Great Britain and you'd like more details, you can contact: Mensa International, 15 The Ivories, 628 Northampton Street, London N1 2NY, England, who will be happy to put you in touch with your own national Mensa organization.

Contents

Introduction 6

Figure Frenzy 8
Figure Frenzy Answers 72

Leaps of Logic 84
Leaps of Logic Answers 120

Mind Marathon 126
Mind Marathon Answers 212

Colour Conundrums 222
Colour Conundrums Answers 250

Introduction

The enormous acclaim given to the first two volumes in this series has encouraged us to produce yet another. Introducing colour into puzzles increases their fascination not only by making them look more interesting, it also enables the puzzle setter to create ever-more perplexing conundrums. Once the colours start to acquire numerical values or symbolic meanings the possibilities are endless. This time we have not only used colour for secret codes and mystery messages but have expanded the scope of the volume by introducing some crosswords with a colour theme and creating a section of mazes that will not only delight the eye but mystify the mind.

For almost a decade the partnership between Mensa and Carlton Books has produced a constant flow of high quality puzzle books that have brought puzzling pleasure to people throughout the world. The humble puzzle book, which was traditionally a rather cheap and tatty object, has become a thing of beauty to display on your coffee table and enjoy with your friends. Our puzzle books have also crossed the language barrier (not such an easy thing to do with puzzles) and helped to enthuse new puzzle fans from as far afield as Poland and Korea.

Robert Allen

Figure Frenzy

Some people just love numbers.

In fact they crunch them the way

others crunch boiled sweets.

This section is for them. It contains

an enormous variety of number

puzzles that will delight even the

most hard-bitten enthusiast. If you're

the sort of person whose best friend

is your pocket calculator, then you may

just have found heaven.

PUZZLE 1

Insert the missing numbers. In each pattern the missing number has something to do with the surrounding numbers in combination.

Answer see page **74**

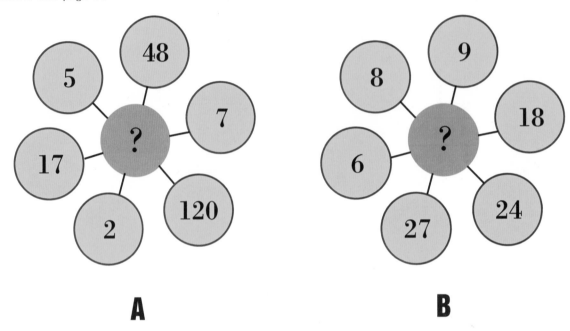

A

B

PUZZLE 2

What number should replace the question mark?

Answer see page **74**

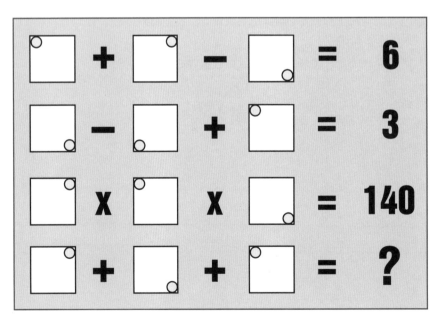

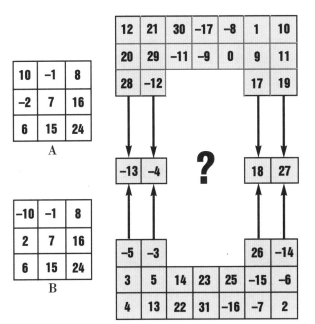

PUZZLE 3

When the shaded sections of this puzzle are brought together, one of the white patches is inserted into the middle to make a magic square in which all rows, columns and long diagonals add to 49.
Is it patch A, B, C or D?

Answer see page **74**

PUZZLE 4

Each shape is made up of two items, and each same shape has the same value, whether in the foreground or background. What number should replace the question mark?

Answer see page **74**

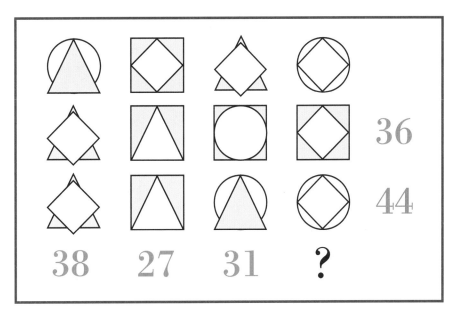

PUZZLE 5

The panel when complete, contains the binary numbers from 1 to 25. Does binary patch A, B, C or D complete the panel?

Answer see page **74**

1	1	0	1	1	1	0	0	1	0	1
1	1	0	1	1	1	1	0	0	0	1
0	0	1	1	0	1	0	1	0	1	1
1	1	0			?			1	1	1
0	1	1						0	0	1
0	0	0						0	1	0
0	1	1	1	0	1	0	0	1	0	1
0	1	1	0	1	1	0	1	0	1	1
1	1	1	0	0	0	1	1	0	0	1

1	0	1	1	1
1	1	1	1	0
1	1	1	0	0

A

0	1	1	0	1
1	1	1	0	0
0	1	0	0	1

B

1	1	0	1	1
1	1	0	1	1
0	0	1	0	1

C

0	1	1	0	1
1	1	1	0	0
1	1	0	0	1

D

PUZZLE 6

Which letters, based on the alphanumeric system, should go into the blank boxes?

Answer see page **74**

6	1	7	3				5	1	3	9				2	2	9	2			
1	3	5	4	A	H	B	2	8	6	4	F	B	C	4	3	0	9			
7	7	0	9				8	6	2	6				7	1	7	8			

PUZZLE 7

What number should replace
the question mark?

Answer see page **74**

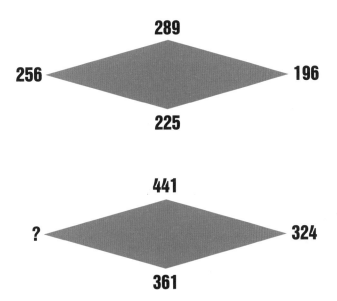

PUZZLE 8

If each large ball weighs one and a third
times the weight of each little ball, what is
the minimum number of balls that need to
be added to the right-hand side to make
the scales balance?

Answer see page **74**

PUZZLE 9

How many rosettes are missing from the blank circle?

Answer see page **74**

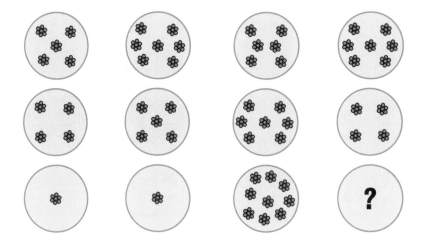

PUZZLE 10

What value needs to go into the upper box to bring this system into balance? Note: The beam is broken down into equal parts and the value of each box is taken from its midpoint.

Answer see page **74**

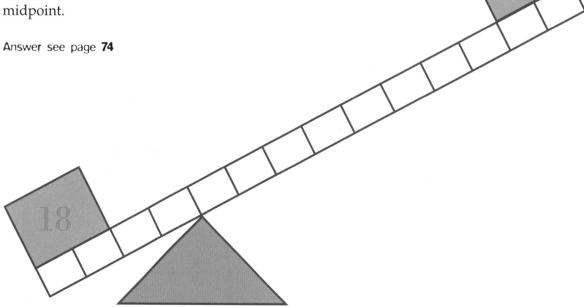

PUZZLE 11

Find a route from the top of this puzzle to the bottom that arrives at the total 353, always going down and to an adjoining hexagon.

Answer see page **74**

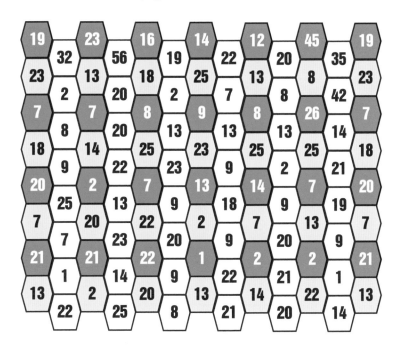

PUZZLE 12

Using only the numbers already used, complete this puzzle to make all the rows, columns, and long diagonals add to 27.

Answer see page **75**

PUZZLE 13

Insert the supplied rows of numbers into the
appropriate places in the grid to make all rows,
columns and long diagonals add to 175.
Example: (C) goes into the location (a).

Answer see page **75**

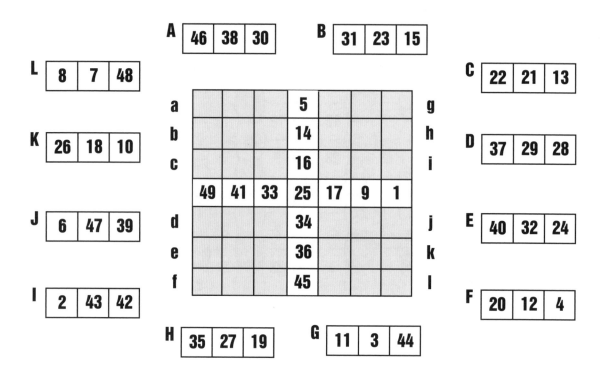

PUZZLE 14

At 3pm one day, a flagpole and
a measuring pole cast shadows
as shown. What length is the
flagpole?

Answer see page **75**

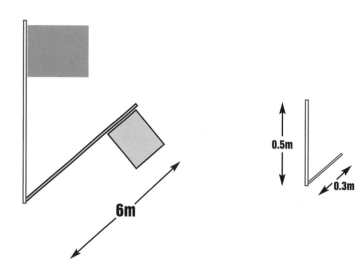

PUZZLE 15

Use logic to discover which shape has the greatest perimeter.

Answer see page **75**

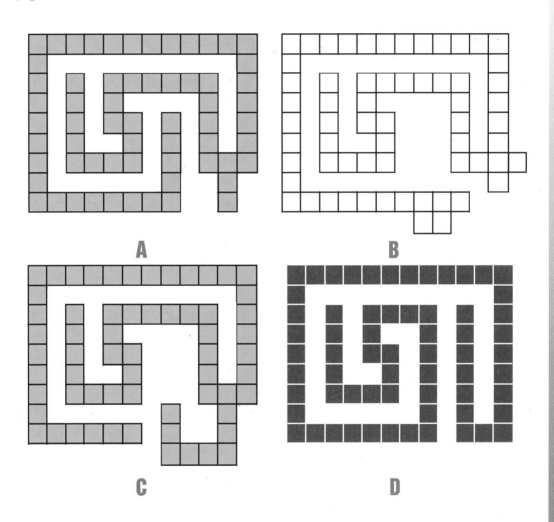

A

B

C

D

A	B	C	D	E	F	G	H	I	J
9	3	8	7	8	9	2	8	5	7
1	2	1	5	?	7	1	0	1	2
K	L	M	N	O	P	Q	R	S	T

PUZZLE 16

Crack the code to find the missing number.

Answer see page **75**

PUZZLE 17

Which number replaces the question mark?
What is the value of each animal?

Answer see page **75**

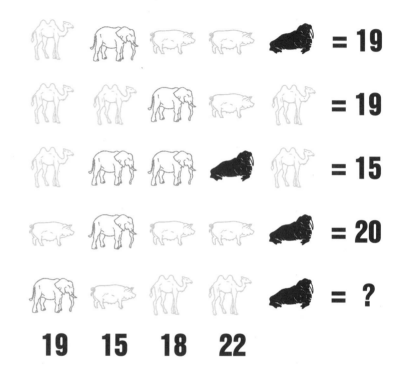

19   15   18   22

PUZZLE 18

Find the missing number.

Answer see page **75**

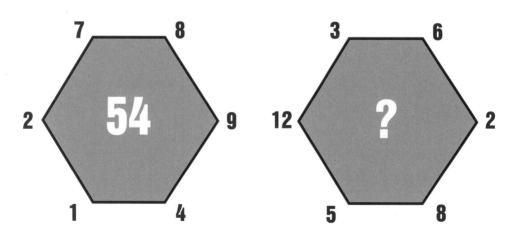

PUZZLE 19

What number should replace the question mark?

Answer see page **75**

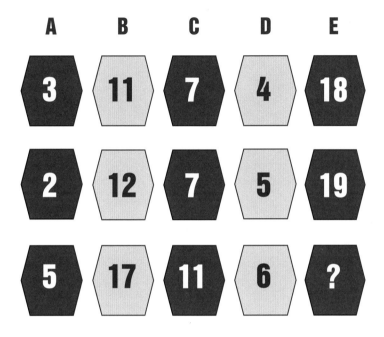

PUZZLE 20

Put the right number in the blank star.

Answer see page **75**

9	4	5	3	6	1	8	2
8	1	2	2	3	2	5	1
6	9	9	1	2	4	3	5
4	8	1	3	5	2	6	1
1	4	3	7	6	3	1	4
9	2	4	8	6	4	5	3
4	2	9	4	8	6	7	1
2	8	1	6	5	9	0	1

PUZZLE 21

Starting from any square on the top row, you can accumulate points by stepping down diagonally to another, adjoining square, and adding that to your total. You may not land on a square containing the number one, or on any square horizontally adjacent to a square with a one, but you may start from such a square. You may not travel up or sideways. By continuing this process until you reach a square on the bottom row, what is the maximum number of points it is possible to accumulate?

Answer see page **75**

PUZZLE 22

When a ball is dropped from a height of 9 m, it bounces back two-thirds of the way. Assuming that the ball comes to rest after making a bounce which takes it less than 2 mm high, how many times does it bounce?

Answer see page **75**

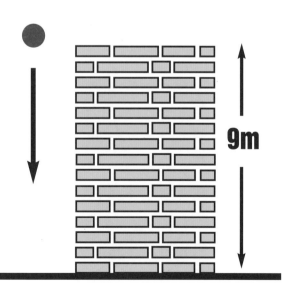

9m

PUZZLE 23

Which number should replace the question mark?

Answer see page 75

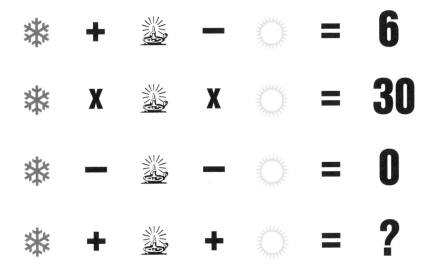

PUZZLE 24

These systems are in balance. What weight is required in the right hand box to balance the load?

Answer see page 75

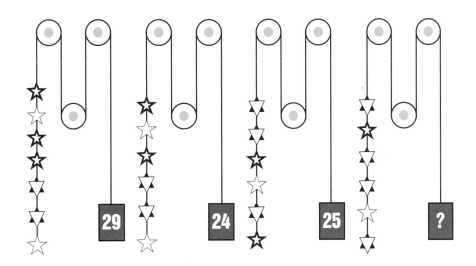

PUZZLE 25

Each like shape has the same value. What number should replace the question mark?

Answer see page **75**

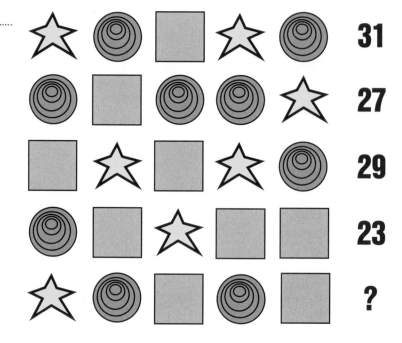

PUZZLE 26

What three-digit number should replace the question mark?

Answer see page **75**

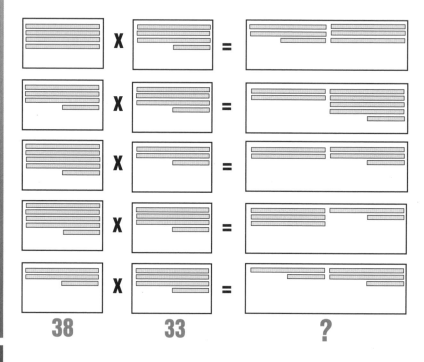

PUZZLE 27

The three balls at the top of each hexagon should contain numbers that, when added together and subtracted from the total of the numbers in the three balls at the bottom of each hexagon, equal the number inside each relevant hexagon. Insert the missing numbers.

Answer see page **76**

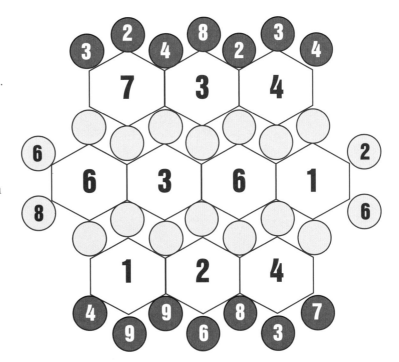

PUZZLE 28

What number should replace the question mark?

Answer see page **76**

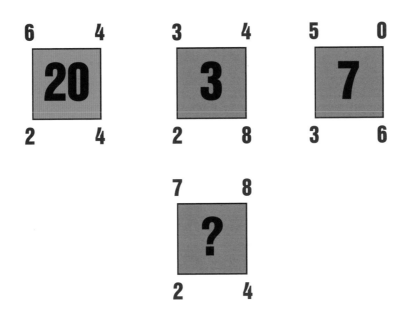

PUZZLE 29

This clock has been designed for a planet that rotates on its axis once every 16 hours. There are 64 minutes to every hour, and 64 seconds to the minute. At the moment, the time on the clock reads a quarter to eight. What time, to the nearest second, will the clock say the time after the next time the hands appear to meet?

Answer see page **76**

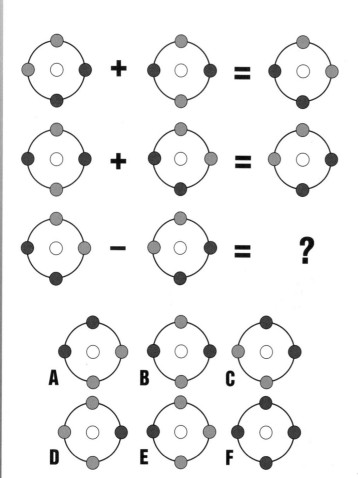

PUZZLE 30

This is a time puzzle. Which symbol is missing? Is it A, B, C, D, E or F?

Answer see page **76**

PUZZLE 31

Which number should replace the question mark?

Answer see page **76**

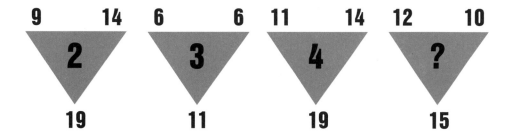

PUZZLE 32

Insert in the boxes at the corner of each shaded number-square, the digits which are multiplied together to give the numbers in the shaded boxes. For example, in the bottom left corner, 144 is derived from 3 x 6 x 8 (and another multiplier – here 1), but you also have to consider how this helps to make solutions for the surrounding numbers… and so on.

Answer see page **76**

3		5		4		4		3		3
	90		120		64		144		54	
2										1
	48		96		16		72		36	
1										2
	160		80		20		150		30	
4										1
	180		10		40		100		15	
9										3
	27		8		32		12		81	
3										9
	24		28		84		45		135	
8										1
	144		42		63		225		25	
3		6		1		3		5		1

PUZZLE 33

What number should replace the question mark?

Answer see page **76**

PUZZLE 34

Each like symbol has the same value.
Supply the missing total.

Answer see page **76**

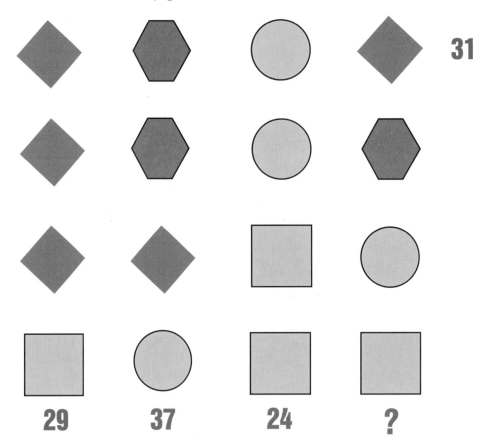

PUZZLE 35

What time will it be, to the nearest second, when the hands of this clock next appear to meet?

Answer see page **76**

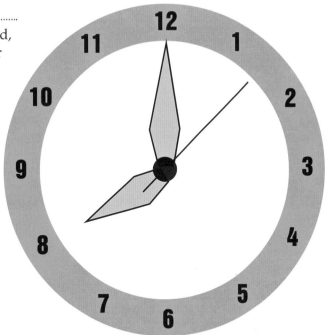

PUZZLE 36

What number should replace the question mark?

Answer see page **76**

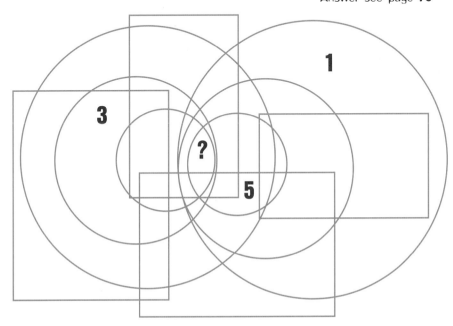

PUZZLE 37

Insert the missing numbers in the blank hexagons.

Answer see page 76

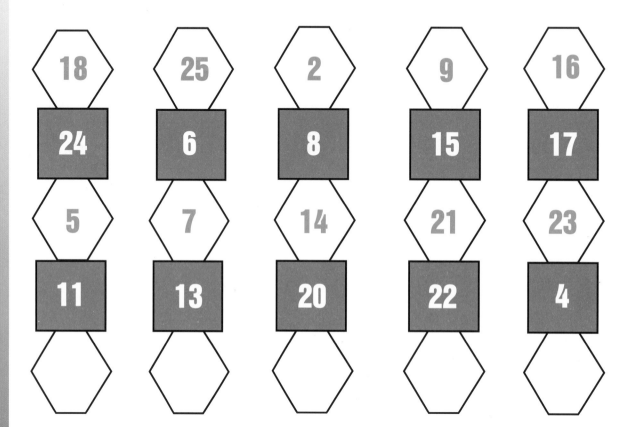

PUZZLE 38

What number should replace the question mark?

Answer see page 77

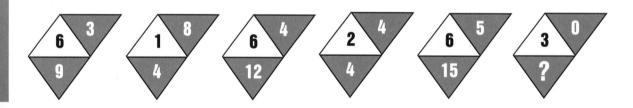

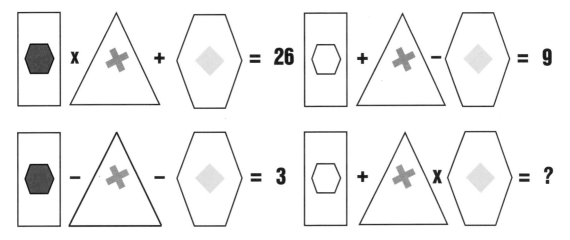

PUZZLE 39

Each like symbol has the same value. What number should replace the question mark?

Answer see page **77**

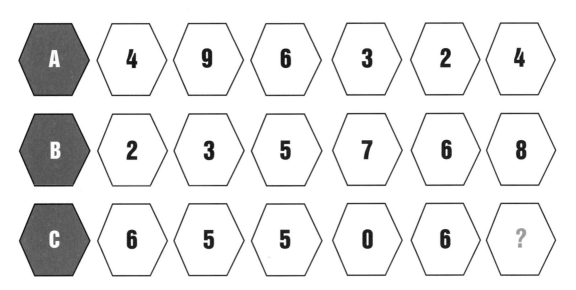

PUZZLE 40

What number should replace the question mark?

Answer see page **77**

PUZZLE 41

What number should replace the question mark in the blank square?

Answer see page **77**

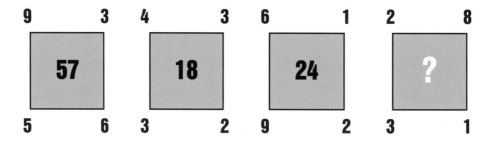

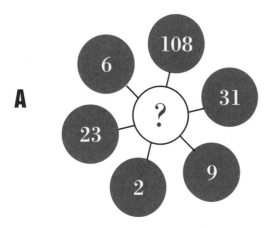

A

PUZZLE 42

Insert the central numbers.

Answer see page **77**

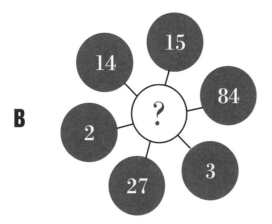

B

PUZZLE 43

The load on this beam and rollers apparatus has to be moved a distance of 20 units. If the circumference of each of the rollers is 0.8 units, how many turns must the rollers make to accomplish the move?

Answer see page **77**

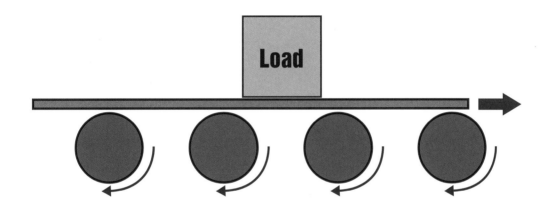

PUZZLE 44

What number should replace the question mark?

Answer see page **77**

PUZZLE 45

The symbols represent the numbers 1 to 9.
Work out the value of the missing
multiplier.

Answer see page **77**

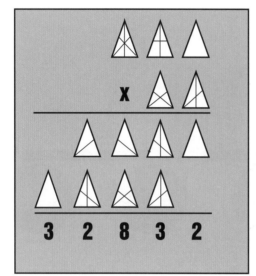 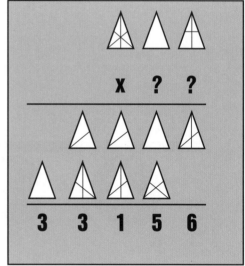

PUZZLE 46

This system is balanced. How heavy is the
black box (ignoring leverage effects)?

Answer see page **77**

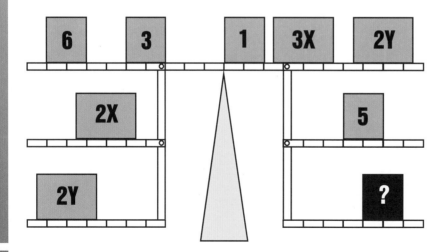

PUZZLE 47

The black, white and shaded rings of this square target always have the same value, irrespective of their position, and each target is worth 44. Which of the targets, A, B, C or D, will replace the question mark?

Answer see page **77**

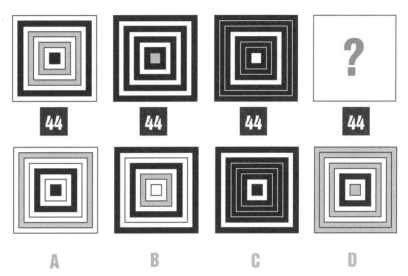

PUZZLE 48

How many different ways is it possible to arrange the order of these four kings?

Answer see page **77**

   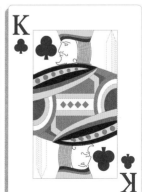

PUZZLE 49

If the top left intersection is worth 1, and the bottom right intersection is worth 25, which of these nodule grids, A, B, C or D, is worth 67?

Answer see page **77**

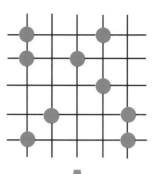

A

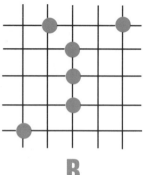

B

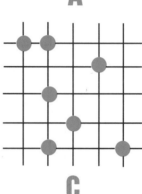

C

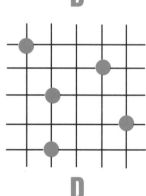

D

PUZZLE 50

Previous to the time shown, when were all four of the digits on this watch last on display?

Answer see page **77**

PUZZLE 51

Each like shape has the same value. Which is the missing symbol?

Answer see page **77**

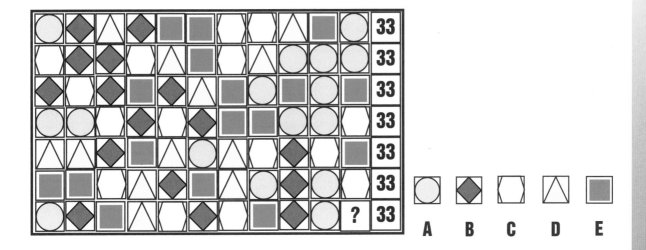

PUZZLE 52

This system is balanced. How heavy is the black weight (ignoring leverage effects)?

Answer see page **77**

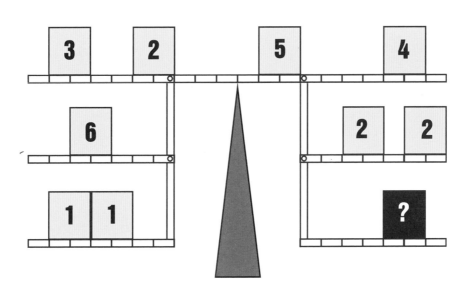

35

PUZZLE 53

There are logical differences in the way each of these squares work, but they all involve simple addition or subtraction of rows. What are the missing numbers?

Answer see page **77**

A

2	6	3	0	8	a
3	8	0	3	9	b
2	3	?	5	7	c
1	9	2	5	4	d
2	1	5	3	6	e

B

2	1	3	2	0	a
1	3	5	6	2	b
0	5	?	4	7	c
2	9	6	3	0	d
1	0	2	9	9	e

C

3	1	2	0	9	a
6	1	4	6	2	b
2	8	?	1	9	c
4	9	6	5	7	d
7	1	3	3	3	e

D

3	3	6	4	7	a
3	3	6	1	1	b
1	1	?	2	0	c
3	4	1	0	6	d
2	1	9	3	2	e

PUZZLE 54

What number should replace the question mark in the third hexagon pattern?

Answer see page **77**

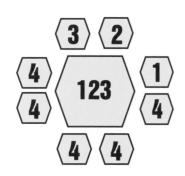

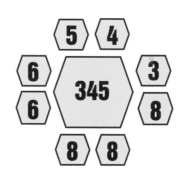

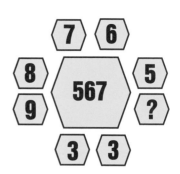

PUZZLE 55

The squares of the times it takes planets to go round their sun are proportional to the cubes of the major axes of their orbits. With this in mind, if CD is four times AB, and a year on the planet Zero lasts for six earth years, how long is a year on the planet Hot?

Answer see page **78**

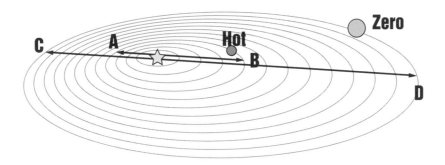

PUZZLE 56

Put the stars into the boxes in such a way that each row is double the row below.

Answer see page **78**

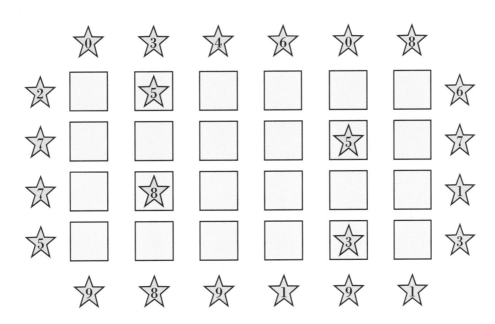

PUZZLE 57

What number should replace the question mark?

Answer see page **78**

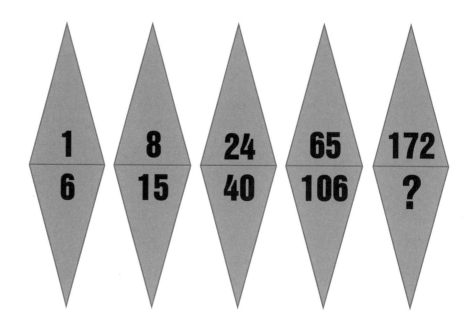

PUZZLE 58

What number should replace the question mark?

Answer see page **78**

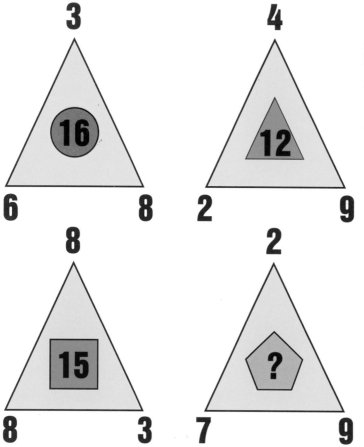

PUZZLE 59

What number should replace
the question mark?

Answer see page **78**

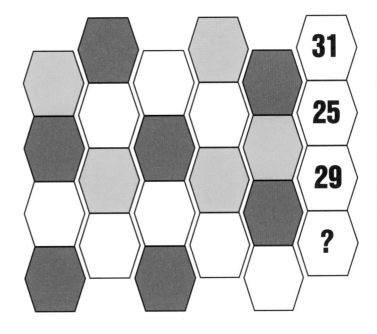

PUZZLE 60

What is the missing number?

Answer see page **78**

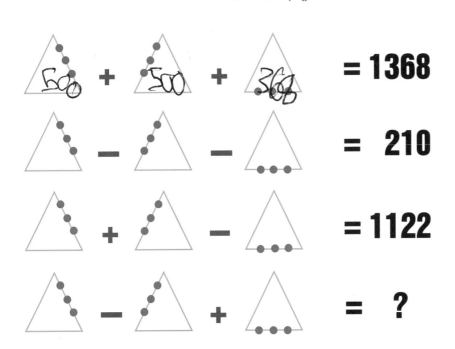

PUZZLE 61

Decode the logic of the puzzle to find the missing number.

Answer see page **78**

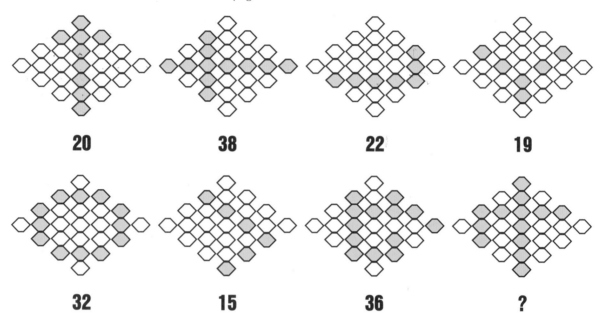

20   **38**   **22**   **19**

32   **15**   **36**   **?**

PUZZLE 62

What is the missing number?

Answer see page **78**

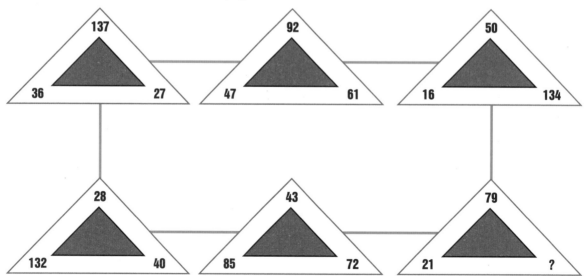

PUZZLE 63

These systems are in balance. What is the missing number?

Answer see page **78**

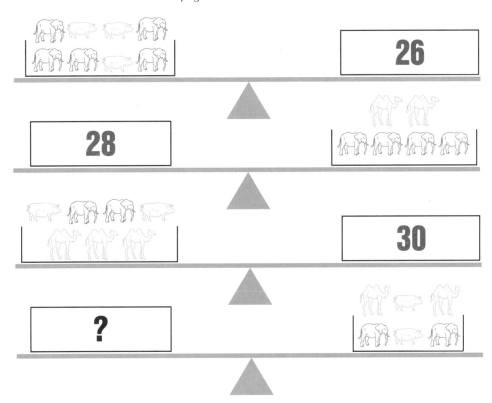

PUZZLE 64

What is the missing number?

Answer see page **78**

27	
9	9
18	

51	
17	39
12	

60	
20	48
12	

45	
15	?
18	

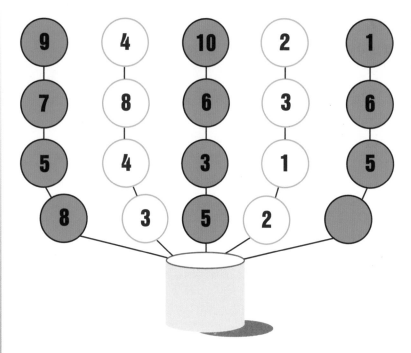

PUZZLE 65

Put the appropriate number on the blank balloon.

Answer see page **78**

PUZZLE 66

Fill in the blanks for Espresso.

Answer see page **78**

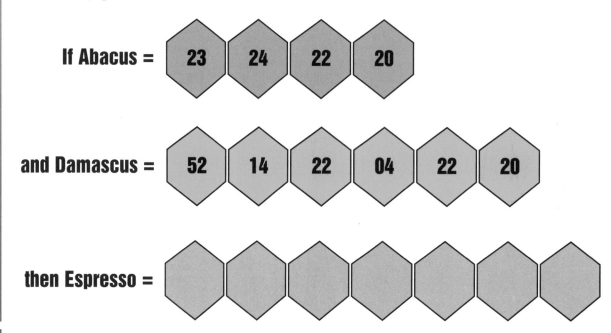

If Abacus = 23 24 22 20

and Damascus = 52 14 22 04 22 20

then Espresso =

PUZZLE 67

What is the missing number?

Answer see page **78**

PUZZLE 68

What is the missing number?

Answer see page **78**

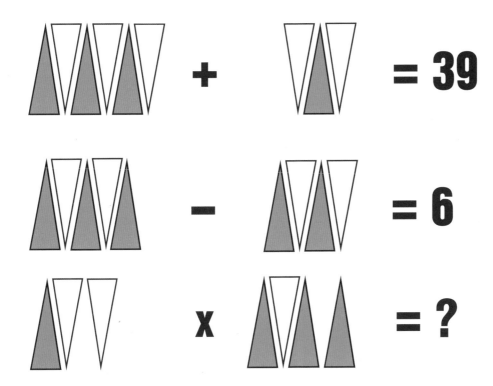

PUZZLE 69

Which of the supplied tiles, A, B, C, D, E or F, logically fits into the vacant space?

Answer see page **79**

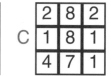

A
8	8	2
2	9	2
4	7	1

B
2	8	2
1	8	1
4	7	2

C
2	8	2
1	8	1
4	7	1

2	9	3	7	3	2	1	1	8	
		5	4	3	8	4	2	4	2	0
8	3	5	6	6	3	0	2	4	
		7	2	9	2	4	1	8	1	4
6	4	7	4	4	2	8	2	4	
		7	2				1	6	1	4
6	2	9	2	6	**?**		2	
		3	9				2	8	2	7
3	4	5	4	8	2	0	1	2	
		2	8	6	3	2	1	8	1	6
2	9	4	6	6	2	4	1	8	
		7	6	8	6	6	4	8	4	2
5	5	9	3	2	2	7	2	5	

D
2	8	2
2	9	2
4	7	1

E
2	8	2
1	9	1
4	5	1

F
3	8	3
1	8	1
4	7	1

PUZZLE 70

Put the appropriate number in the blank triangle.

Answer see page **79**

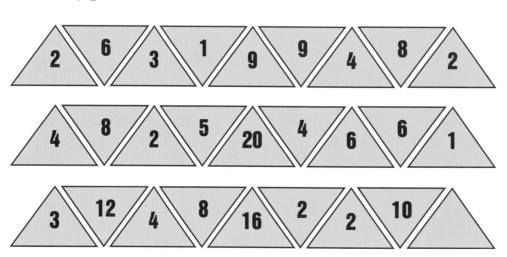

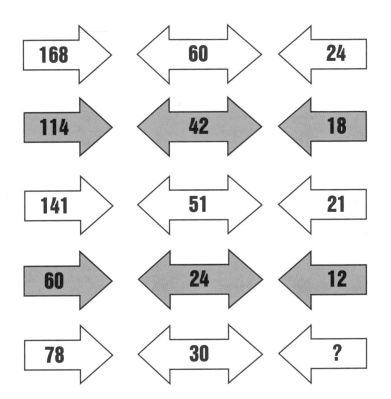

PUZZLE 71

What is the missing number?

Answer see page **79**

PUZZLE 72

In the blank hexagon at the corner of each black box, write a single-digit number which, when added to the other three corner numbers, equals the total in the middle. For example, 25 could be 5 + 5 + 6 + 9. But you have to consider how the surrounding totals, 20, 19, and 21, will be affected by your choice. You must use each digit – including 0 – at least once.

Answer see page **79**

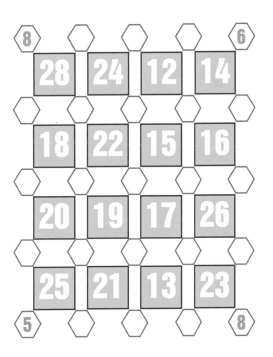

PUZZLE 73

Complete the analogy.

Answer see page **79**

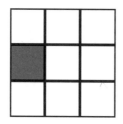 is to **6** as 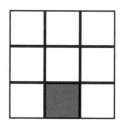 is to **?**

PUZZLE 74

Fill the numbers into the blank spaces.
There is only one correct way.

Answer see page **79**

ACROSS

118	2133	6289
126	2345	6321
149	2801	9134
197	2803	9277
421	3458	9783
738	3482	12304
769	3485	12334
823	4190	12345
864	4227	53802
932	4656	56182
987	5199	0693878
1366	5660	9124914

DOWN

14	8228	443628
15	9998	492660
25	12735	536293
33	15787	593680
39	17151	4143383
42	24991	5428292
1178	26114	6132104
2119	64843	586713226
3002	116357	981921603
6334	200900	

PUZZLE 75

The only symbols that concern you in this multiplication puzzle are stars. Using their positions on the grid, calculate the missing number.

Answer see page **79**

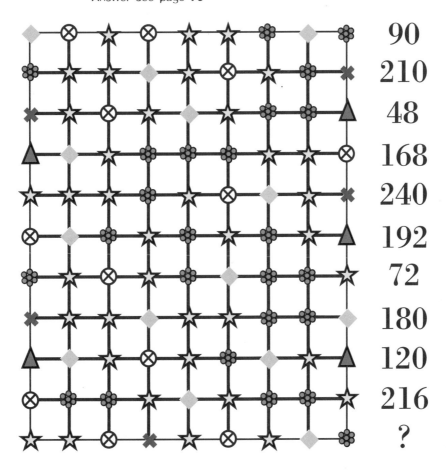

90
210
48
168
240
192
72
180
120
216
?

PUZZLE 76

Fill in the blank squares.

Answer see page **79**

PUZZLE 77

What is the missing number?

Answer see page 79

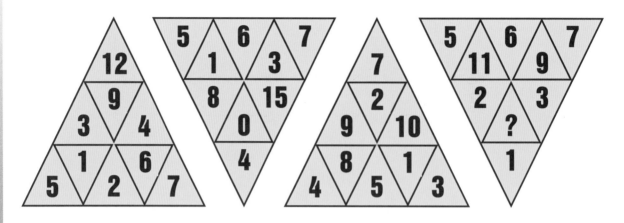

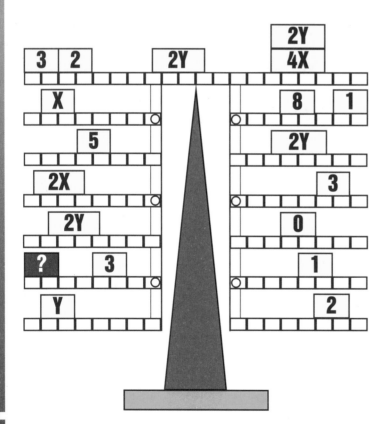

PUZZLE 78

This system is balanced.
How heavy is the purple box
(ignoring leverage effects)?

Answer see page 79

PUZZLE 79

Each like shape has the same value. Which shape should replace the question mark?

Answer see page **80**

PUZZLE 80

What is the value of the right-hand target?

Answer see page **80**

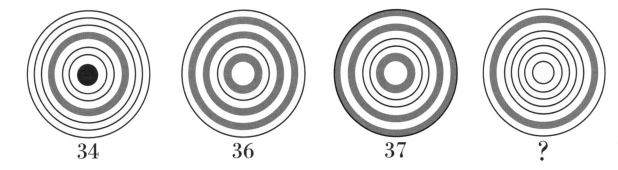

PUZZLE 81

What is the missing number?

Answer see page **80**

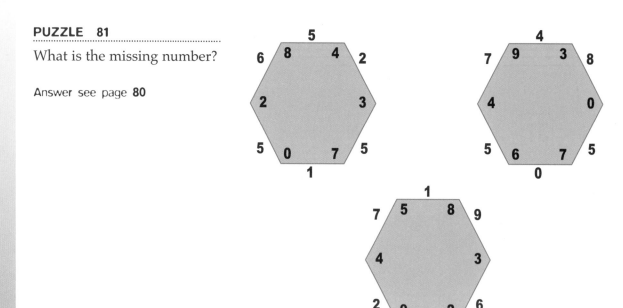

PUZZLE 82

The numbers in the three balls above each cell, when multiplied together, minus the value of the numbers in the three balls below each cell, when multiplied together, is equal to the value of the numbers inside each cell. Insert the missing numbers.

Answer see page **80**

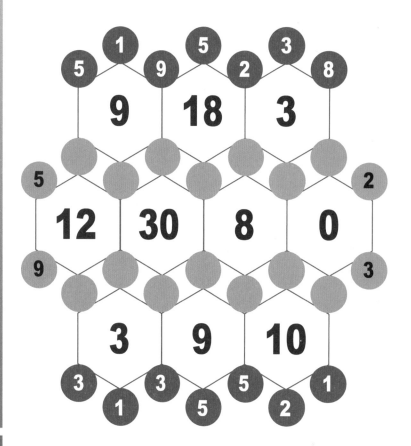

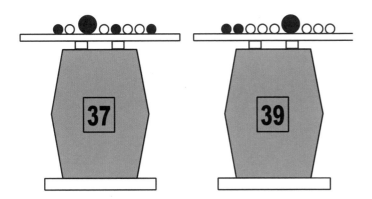

PUZZLE 83

If each large ball weighs three units, what is the weight of each small black ball? A small white ball has a different weight from a small black ball. All small balls are solid; both the large balls are hollow.

Answer see page **80**

PUZZLE 84

Each like symbol has the same value. What number should replace the question mark?

Answer see page **80**

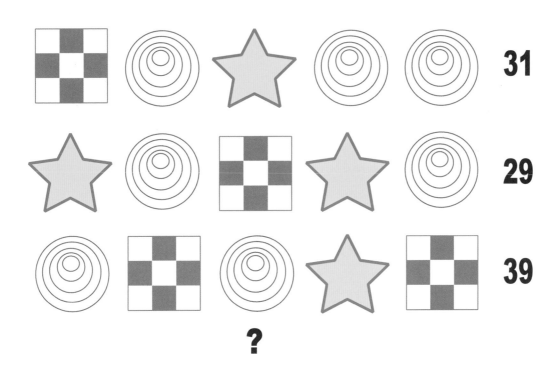

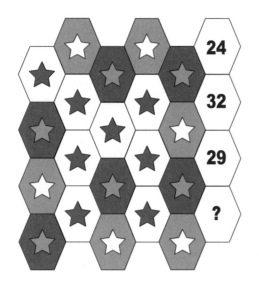

PUZZLE 85

What is the missing number?

Answer see page **80**

PUZZLE 86

Fill the numbers into the grid. They only fit one way.

Answer see page **80**

ACROSS

69	263	726	1761670
76	328	751	4256701
84	338	758	4971467
97	447	778	5231937
092	450	821	6368906
096	472	847	6579804
101	517	930	6596817
122	627	957	7062502
131	650	974	7554403
147	660	0379304	8369591
167	692	1062387	9511198
171	697	1291762	9512209
178	706	1518117	9974515
239	711	1751171	

DOWN

069	298915	1028507	7081701
106	412961	1508171	7097230
352	497811	1970788	7097429
353	517268	2567039	7121176
379	576816	3374277	7364561
461	584605	3602976	7607138
513	709656	4298164	7632154
573	720412	4650786	7948137
590	797991	5247127	8076467
126959	862178	7057147	9912061
162717			

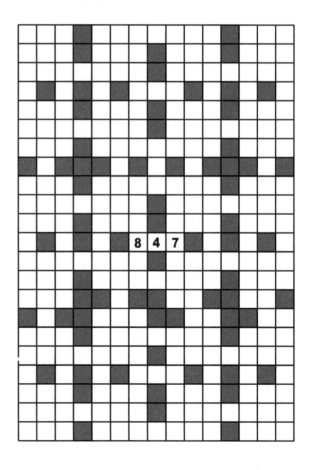

PUZZLE 87

Put a value from below into each triangle so that the total in each square gives a value that makes each row, column, and long diagonal add to 203.

Answer see page **80**

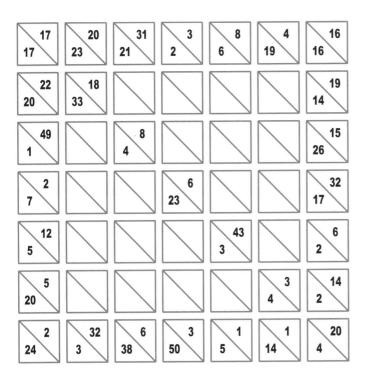

6 8 29 9 27 30 13
7 3 29 14 15 8 3
2 19 11 12 39 0
40 1 7 11 2 9 2
34 13 10 8 12 20
19 36 5 4 5 18 40

PUZZLE 88

Insert the missing number in the blank square.

Answer see page **81**

9	8
1	2

4	0
2	5

6	2
4	

5	5
4	9

8	2
3	4

7	1
2	3

PUZZLE 89

What is the missing number?

Answer see page 81

PUZZLE 90

Decode the logic of the puzzle to find the missing number.

Answer see page 81

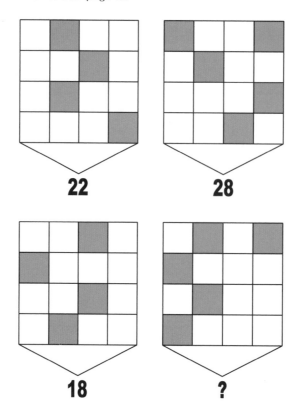

PUZZLE 91

What are the individual values of the dark blue, white and shaded hexagons?

Answer see page **81**

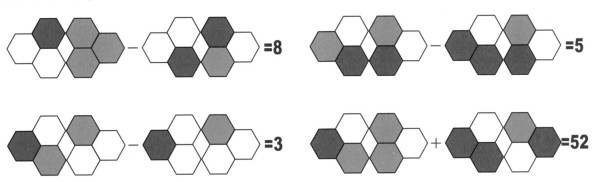

```
1 0 2 2 4 9 3 8 4 7 4 6 0 9 8 7 1 2 3 4 5 4 6 6 8 8 3 4 7 1 2 9 4 8 8 7 6 2 5 5 4 5
4 4 7 0 0 1 1 2 3 1 3 5 0 1 5 7 6 1 2 0 8 6 9 2 5 2 8 1 8 0 2 7 9 5 3 9 8 7 0 9 1
7 2 9 3 5 3 8 9 2 0 1 0 2 6 0 3 9 1 6 7 0 7 1 7 6 9 8 1 5 9 9 5 6 5 0 3 2 9 0 0 3 0
7 2 9 1 8 0 7 7 8 0 7 6 9 7 8 5 3 2 6 0 8 9 2 9 9 1 2 0 2 9 1 7 0 7 7 1 9 7 8 3 0 0
9 1 0 3 2 5 0 5 2 5 1 6 7 2 8 9 6 2 9 0 9 6 0 9 1 3 8 5 0 7 9 9 0 9 8 5 0 3 2 9 1 0
9 9 1 0 7 8 2 7 3 6 4 5 6 9 7 0 8 2 3 6 5 5 4 2 3 1 0 9 8 4 6 7 3 9 2 9 0 9 0 4 6 2 2
```

PUZZLE 92

Somewhere within the number above, there is a number which, if put into the grid below, starting at the top left and working from left to right, row by row, will have the middle column as shown when the grid is completed. Put in the missing numbers.

Answer see page **81**

					4					
					1					
					8					
					9					
					1					
					6					
					0					
					8					
					1					
					2					
					9					
					2					

PUZZLE 93

Complete the analogy.

Answer see page **81**

is to 24 as   is to 28 as   is to ?

PUZZLE 94

Only the value of the positions of the coloured boxes in each column are added to give the number at the bottom (the numbers in the white boxes are a further clue). Work out the logic to find the value of the question mark.

Answer see page **81**

13											24
											25
37											
											49
61											
84											73
108	114	126	185	66	141	140	150	156	119	171	?

PUZZLE 95

What is the missing number?

Answer see page **81**

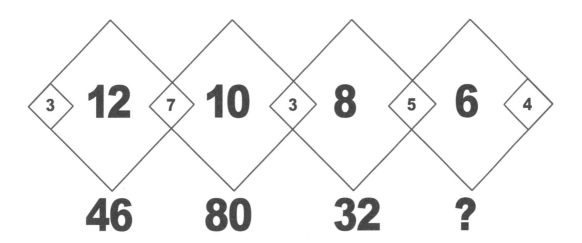

46   80   32   ?

PUZZLE 96

Which of these four sets is the odd one out?

Answer see page **81**

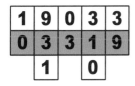

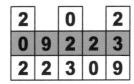

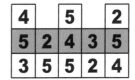

A   B   C   D

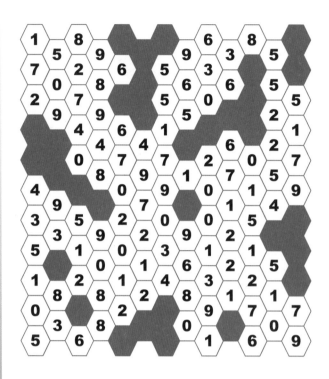

PUZZLE 97

Find a route from the top to the bottom of this puzzle that gives 175 as a total. Any number adjacent to a zero reduces your total to zero.

Answer see page **81**

PUZZLE 98

How many bacteria cultures should be in the Petri dish with the question mark?

Answer see page **81**

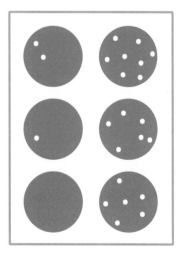

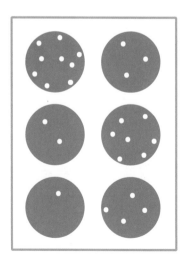

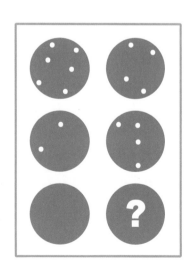

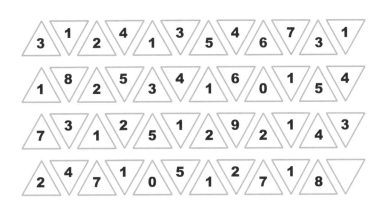

PUZZLE 99

Insert the appropriate value in the blank triangle.

Answer see page **81**

PUZZLE 100

What is the missing number?

Answer see page **81**

PUZZLE 101

Each like symbol has the same value.
Work out the value of the missing digit.

Answer see page **82**

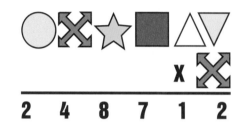

2   4   8   7   1   2

7   4   6   1   3   6

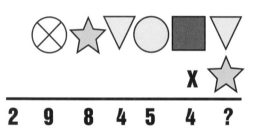

2   9   8   4   5   4   ?

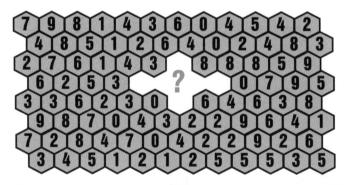

PUZZLE 102

Which block of cells fits
logically into the space?

Answer see page **82**

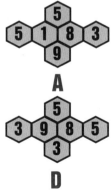

A

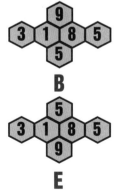

B

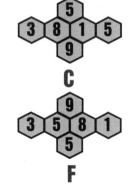

C

D

E

F

PUZZLE 103

How many revolutions per minute
does the small wheel make?

Answer see page **82**

? rev / minute

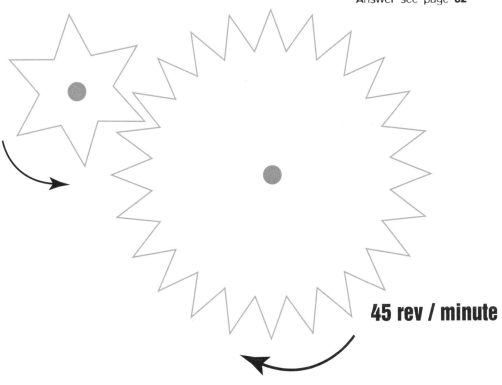

45 rev / minute

PUZZLE 104

What is the missing point value?

Answer see page **82**

PUZZLE 105

Use three straight lines to divide this square into five sections, each of which contains a total value of 60.

Answer see page **82**

```
1   9   3   7       1       4   9   3
    7   9   8       3   0 3     3   5   9
        7       0       0     1       7
    8       5       1         0
        0       1   1     1             7
            0   5       4       6     2
    2                       0   6     0
    8               7   7       2       9
            9       3           8   3
        3           4       7   0
                    9
            1                       1   7
    2       0       4       3   6
        8       1       2             3
    1       5       7       0   5   3
        5       4       4       2   2   9
                                2
```

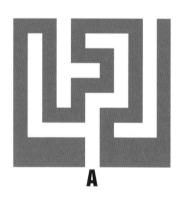

A

B

PUZZLE 106

Use logic to find which shape has the greatest perimeter.

Answer see page **82**

C

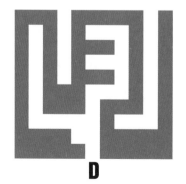

D

PUZZLE 107

Supply both the missing numbers.

Answer see page **82**

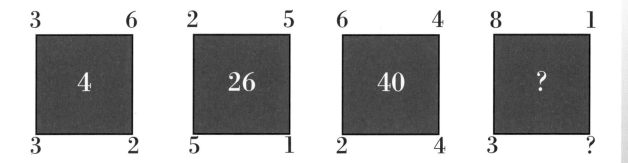

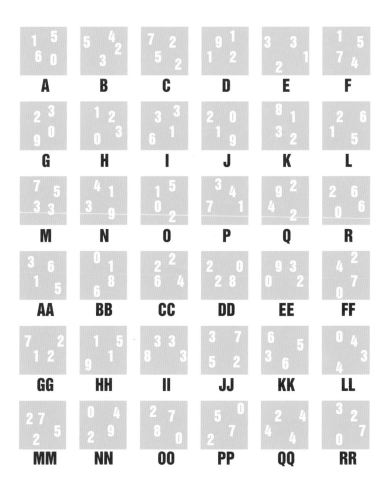

PUZZLE 108

Find the block in each row which, when you multiply the highest two numbers together, and add the other two digits in the block to the product to arrive at a solution, then add the solutions from the chosen blocks in the other rows together, will give you the highest possible total. Repeat the process to also find the lowest possible total.

Answer see page **82**

PUZZLE 109

Find hidden within the stars, a long multiplication sum with a six-figure result.

Answer see page **82**

PUZZLE 110

Make an exact quarter using all these numbers, and no other.

Answer see page **82**

2 5 2 5 2 5 2 5 0

PUZZLE 111

The values represented by the black segments surrounding each number are processed in two stages to get the numbers in the middle of each system. Find the missing number.

Answer see page **83**

PUZZLE 112

What is the missing profit figure?

Answer see page **83**

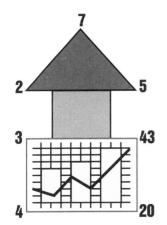

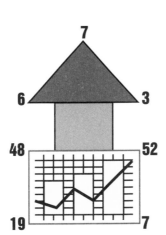

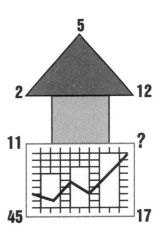

65

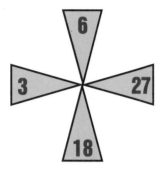

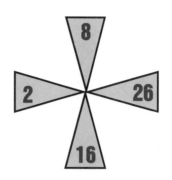

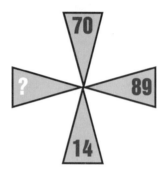

PUZZLE 113

Which number replaces the question mark?

Answer see page **83**

PUZZLE 114

Fill the numbers into the blank spaces. There is only one correct way.

Answer see page **83**

ACROSS

30	326	649	2768259
74	359	659	4346540
87	386	691	5783968
93	390	697	6281307
018	467	721	6445535
042	496	735	6490916
133	516	929	6906308
148	519	954	7590936
273	563	989	9473460
298	619		9798259
306			

DOWN

043	928	2369674	7533652
192	165263	3268959	7934895
313	320469	4906736	9219367
333	372108	5176453	9452695
344	697469	5364749	9497059
460	0840396	6089148	9687097
521	0929969	7485571	9759968
863			

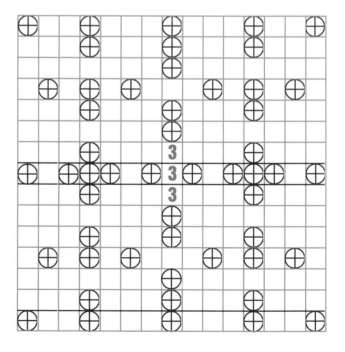

PUZZLE 115

Discover the vital relationship between all of these numbers to find the missing number.

Answer see page **83**

41
2   23
11

43
3   29
13

47
5   31
17

53
7   37
?

PUZZLE 116

What is the value of the target on the right?

Answer see page **83**

33

45

34

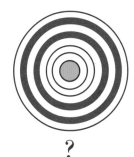

?

PUZZLE 117

This system is balanced. How heavy is the black box (ignoring leverage effects)?

Answer see page **83**

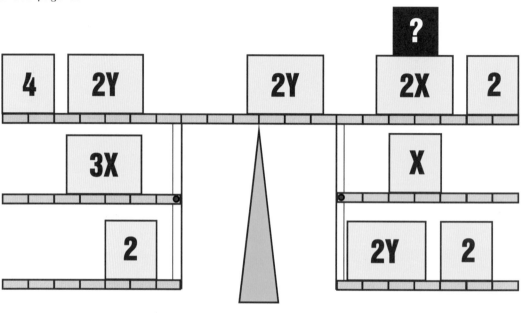

PUZZLE 118

Put digits in the squares above and below each diamond and multiply them together. Do the same with the numbers to the left and right of each diamond and subtract the lower result from the higher to obtain the middle numbers.

Answer see page **83**

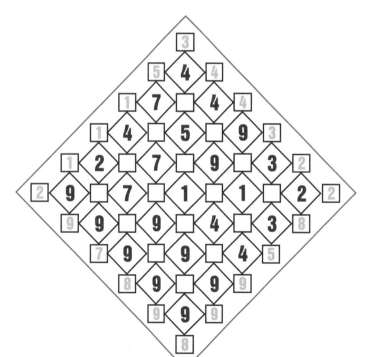

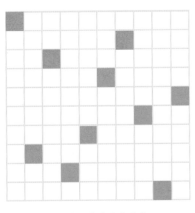

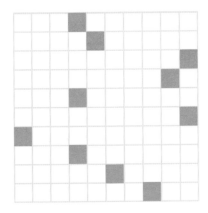

0324924831

3591300652

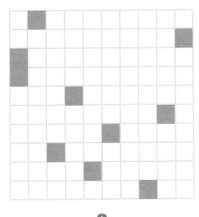

?

PUZZLE 119

What is the missing value of this logic series?

Answer see page **83**

PUZZLE 120

Complete the analogy.

Answer see page **83**

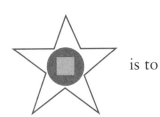 is to  as **186681** is to ?

861168   **166881**   **168861**   **816618**   **681186**
   A   **B**   **C**   **D**   **E**

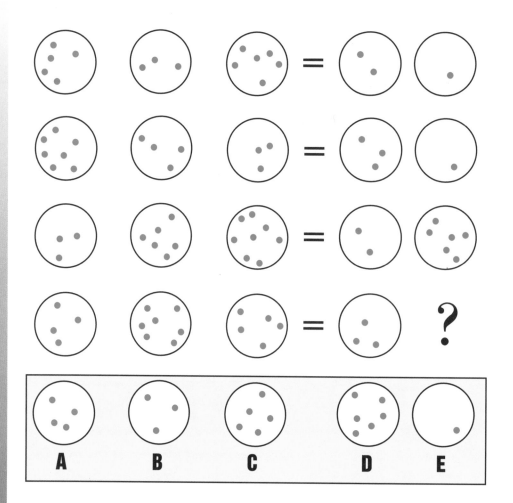

PUZZLE 121

Which Petri dish of bacteria cultures
should replace the question mark?

Answer see page **83**

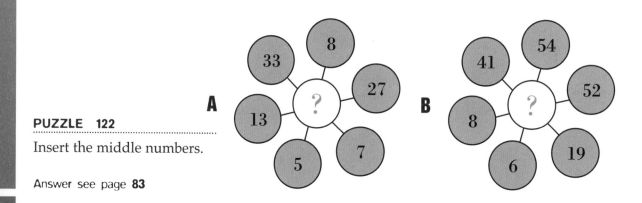

PUZZLE 122

Insert the middle numbers.

Answer see page **83**

PUZZLE 123

What is the missing number in this sequence?

Answer see page **83**

PUZZLE 124

Insert the rows into the appropriate places in the grid to make all lines, columns, and long diagonals add to 105.

Answer see page **83**

| 27 | 25 | 16 |

| -2 | -4 | 36 |

| 14 | 5 | 3 |

| 18 | 9 | 0 |

| 2 | -7 | 33 |

| -6 | 34 | 32 |

| 19 | 17 | 8 |

| 38 | 29 | 20 |

| -3 | 37 | 28 |

| 10 | 1 | -8 |

| 22 | 13 | 11 |

| 30 | 21 | 12 |

Grid:
		39			
		31			
		23			
35	26	24	15	6	4	-5
		7			
		-1			
		-9			

Figure Frenzy

Answers

Answer 1
A. 24. Opposite numbers are divided or added to give 24.
B. 3. Opposite numbers are multiplied or divided by 3.

Answer 2
16.

Answer 3
D. This is the only patch that works for all the lines.

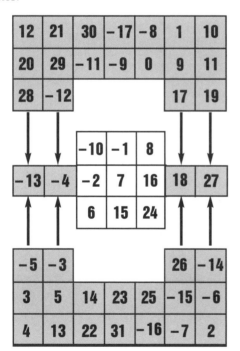

Answer 4
25.
Circle = 4
Triangle = 8
Diamond = 5
Square = 2
The values are added when the shapes are combined.

Answer 5
D. The binary numbers start at the top and work left to right, line by line.

1	1	0	1	1	1	0	0	1	0	1
1	1	0	1	1	1	1	0	0	0	1
0	0	1	1	0	1	0	1	0	1	1
1	1	0	0	1	1	0	1	1	1	1
0	1	1	1	1	1	0	0	0	0	1
0	0	0	1	1	0	0	1	0	1	0
0	1	1	1	0	1	0	0	1	0	1
0	1	1	0	1	1	0	1	0	1	1
1	1	1	0	0	0	1	1	0	0	1

Answer 6
E, G, G. These represent the number 577, which is added to the sum of the previous top and middle line, to get the bottom line.

Answer 7
400. The numbers are the squares of 14 to 21 inclusive.

Answer 8
5 (4 big and 1 little).

Answer 9
3. Add the rosettes and take the middle line from the top line.

Answer 10
6. The right weight is nine units across to balance the left three units across. 6 x 9 (54) balances 18 x 3 (54).

Answer 11
Follow this route.

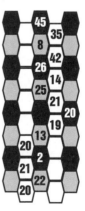

Answer 12

6	2	9	3	7
3	7	6	2	9
2	9	3	7	6
7	6	2	9	3
9	3	7	6	2

Answer 13

22	21	13	5	46	38	30
31	23	15	14	6	47	39
40	32	24	16	8	7	48
49	41	33	25	17	9	1
2	43	42	34	26	18	10
11	3	44	36	35	27	19
20	12	4	45	37	29	28

Answer 14

10 m. The ratio of the flagpole to its shadow is the same as the ratio of the measuring stick to its shadow.

Answer 15

D. The least number of faces touching each other gives the greatest perimeter.

Answer 16

1. A + B = KL, C + D = MN, and so on.

Answer 17

18.
Elephant = 2
Walrus = 3
Camel = 4
Pig = 5

Answer 18

78. Multiply opposite numbers and add the results to get the numbers in the middle. Thus 24 + 24 + 30 = 78.

Answer 19

28. Each row is a sequence of
A + D = C, D + C = B and B + C = E.

Answer 20

6. Add the value of the top two stars of each column to value of the middle two stars to get the value of the bottom two stars.

Answer 21

46 points, taking this route:

9	4	5	3	6	1	8	2
8	1	2	2	3	2	5	1
6	9	9	1	2	4	3	5
4	8	1	3	5	2	6	1
1	4	3	7	6	3	1	4
9	2	4	8	6	4	5	3
4	2	9	4	8	6	7	1
2	8	1	6	5	9	0	1

Answer 22

21 times.

Answer 23

10.
Snowflake = 5
Candle = 3
Sun = 2

Answer 24

24. The pieces have the following values:

☆ = 5

✡ = 4

☆ = 3

Answer 25

25. Star = 9, Whorl = 5, Square = 3

Answer 26

248. Long lines = 2, short lines = 1. Add the values on the right to arrive at the answer.

Answer 27

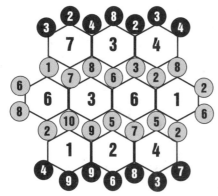

Answer 28

27. The bottom two digits expressed as a number, subtracted from the top two digits, also expressed as a number. The difference is halved and the result is put in the middle. 78 – 24 = 54. 54 ÷ 2 = 27.

Answer 29

9 minutes and 9 seconds after 1.

Answer 30

B. The shaded spots represent the hands of a clock. 3:00 – 9:00 = 6:00.

Answer 31

7. Take the middle number from the top left number. Multiply that by 2 to get the top right number. Add 5 to the top right number to get the bottom number.

Answer 32

3		5		4		4		3		3
	90		120		64		144		54	
2		3		2		2		6		1
	48		96		16		72		36	
1		8		2		2		3		2
	160		80		20		150		30	
4		5		1		5		5		1
	180		10		40		100		15	
9		1		2		4		1		3
	27		8		32		12		81	
3		1		4		1		3		9
	24		28		84		45		135	
8		1		7		3		5		1
	144		42		63		225		25	
3		6		1		3		5		1

Answer 33

42. The bottom number goes next to the top one to make a two-digit number; the left and right do the same. Then subtract the second number from the first.
96 – 54 = 42.

Answer 34

32.
Diamond = 7
Circle = 4
Hexagon = 13
Square = 8

Answer 35

38 seconds after 8.43.

Answer 36

7. There are 7 areas of intersection at this position.

Answer 37

12, 19, 26, 3, 10. The bottom line of a Magic Square, in which all rows, columns, and long diagonals equal 70.

Answer 38

0. The top two numbers are multiplied in shapes 1, 3 and 5. The answers are put as single-digit numbers in the top triangles of shapes 2, 4 and 6. In all the shapes the top two numbers are multiplied, then halved, 3 x 0 = 0.

Answer 39

22.
Rectangle = 8
Triangle = 3
Hexagon = 2

Answer 40

2. C = A – B, with the result reversed. 496324 – 235768 = 260556.

Answer 41

19. The top pair of numbers are multiplied together and added to the result of multiplying the bottom pair of numbers together. (2 x 8) + (3 x 1).

Answer 42

A. 54, B. 42. Opposite numbers are multiplied, divided, or added to get the numbers in the middle.

Answer 43

12½ turns. For every unit that the rollers cover, the beam is pushed two units.

Answer 44

1. The number is an anagram of Mensa, with numbers substituted for the letters.

Answer 45

36.

```
  912        921
x  36      x  36
 5472       5526
 2736       2763
32832      33156
```

Answer 46

3 units. The difference of 24 divided by 8.

Answer 47

C.
White = 7
Black = 5
Shaded = 3

Answer 48

24 ways. There are six alternatives with each suit at the left.

Answer 49

B. Each nodule is given a value, depending on its position in the grid. The values are added together.

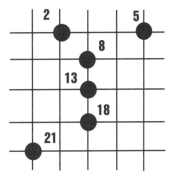

Answer 50

15:03 (or 03.15 (pm) if the watch has the capacity to switch to 12-hour mode).

Answer 51

A.
Circle = 1
Diamond = 4
Square = 3
Triangle = 2
Hexagon = 5

Answer 52

2. The weight is positioned 8 units along, so it needs a weight of 2 units (8 x 2 = 16) to keep the system in balance.

Answer 53

A = 5. (a + b) – (d + e) = c
B = 0. (d + e) – (a + b) = c
C = 3. (d + e) - (a + b) = c
D = 2. (a + b) - (d + e) = c

Answer 54

2. The top four numbers, plus the number in the middle, equals the bottom four numbers. Hence 8765 + 567 = 9332.

Answer 55
9 earth months (6 earth years divided by 8).

Answer 56

Answer 57
279. The numbers are added together and the sum + 1 is put in the next triangle. 106 + 172 = 278 + 1 + 279

Answer 58
13. Add all the digits together and subtract the number of sides of the central figure.

Answer 59
19.
Shaded = 9
Blue = 5
White = 3

Answer 60
456. The first symbols are worth 789; the middle symbols are worth 456; the right-hand symbols are worth 123.

Answer 61
35. White hexagons have no value. Yellow hexagons are worth 1 in the top row, 2 in the second row, 3 in the third row, 4 in the fourth row, then 3 in the fifth row, 2 in the sixth row and 1 in the seventh row.

Answer 62
100. The numbers inside each triangle total 200.

Answer 63
24.
Elephant = 4
Pig = 2
Camel = 6

Answer 64
27. The left number is one-third of the top and the right is subtracted from the top number to give the bottom.

Answer 65
4. In each row, the numbers in the two left balloons equal the numbers in the three right balloons.

Answer 66

Move one place to the right in the alphabet. A=2, B=3. The numbers to make espresso are E=6, S=20, P=17, R=19 and O=16.

Answer 67
30. Multiply the top two numbers together and the bottom two numbers together. Then subtract the lower from the higher and then put answer in the middle. This is done continuously.
(12 x 7) [84] – (9 x 6) [54] = 30.

Answer 68
252.
Red triangle = 6
White triangle = 3
12 x 21 = 252.

Answer 69

C. The 1st and 2nd numbers in each line, multiplied together, equal the last two numbers. The 3rd and 4th numbers multiplied together, equal the 6th and 7th. The 6th and 7th numbers minus the 8th and 9th numbers equal the 5th number of each line.

Answer 70

5. Each line contains three separate multiplication sums with the answer in between the multipliers. $10 \div 2 = 5$.

Answer 71

14. Divide the left number by 3 and add 4 to give the middle number. Repeat the sums with the middle number to get the right number. $78 \div 3 = 26$; $26 + 4 = 30$; $30 \div 3 = 10$; $10 + 4 = 14$.

Answer 72

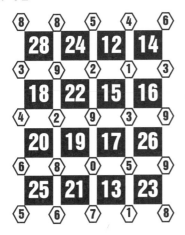

Answer 73

8. The squares are numbered from 1 to 9, starting on the top left, from left to right, right to left, left to right.

Answer 74

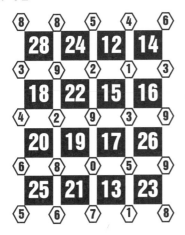

Answer 75

70. Each star is valued from 1 to 9, depending on its position in the columns from the left of each row. The values are then multiplied. The stars appear in columns 1, 2, 5 and 7, so the sums are: $1 \times 2 (2) \times 5 (10) \times 7 = 70$.

Answer 76

425. Reverse the top line, subtract the second line from that, and subtract the result from the bottom line to get the three figure sum for the blanks.
$6130 - 2589 = 3541$; $3966 - 3541 = 425$.

Answer 77

5. The numbers in all the triangles add up to 49.

Answer 78

2 units. The difference of 16 divided by 8. The units to the right come to 104, to the left they are 86. $104 - 86 = 18$. The blank box is 9 units across so $2 \times 9 = 18$.

Answer 79

B. The values of the shapes are:

 = 5

 = 2

 = 6

 = 4

 = 3

Answer 80

31.
White ring = 4
Blue ring = 6
Shaded ring = 3

Answer 81

6. In each case, the sum of the numbers outside a hexagon equals the sum of the numbers inside it.

Answer 82

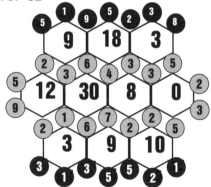

Answer 83

Small black balls weigh 6 units. White balls weigh 4 units.

Answer 84

21.
Whorl = 5
Chequered box = 13
Star = 3

Answer 85

27.
Shaded hexagon / white star = 3
Blue hexagon / shaded star = 5
White hexagon / black star = 8

Answer 86

3	3	8		7	5	5	4	4	0	3		4	4	7
6	5	0		6	9	2		2	6	3		6	6	0
0	3	7	9	3	0	4		9	9	7	4	5	1	5
2		6		2		7	7	8		4		0		7
9	7	4		1	7	1		1	2	2		7	1	1
7	0	6	2	5	0	2		6	5	7	9	8	0	4
6	9	7		4	9	7	1	4	6	7		6	2	7
	7				7		0		7				8	
1	4	7		4	2	5	6	7	0	1		7	5	8
5	2	3	1	9	3	7		6	3	6	8	9	0	6
0	9	6		7	0	6		0	9	2		4	7	2
8		4		8		8	4	7		7		8		1
1	7	5	1	1	7	1		1	5	1	8	1	1	7
7	2	6		1	0	6	2	3	8	7		3	2	8
1	0	1			9			8	4			7	6	
	4			1	6	7			6	9			9	7
5	1	7		9	5	1	2	2	0	9		4	5	0
1	2	9	1	7	6	2		9	5	1	1	1	9	8
7		7		0		1	7	8		2		2	1	
2	3	9		7	5	1		9	3	0		9	5	7
6	5	9	6	8	1	7		1	7	6	1	6	7	0
8	2	1		8	3	6	9	5	9	1		1	3	1

Answer 87

17/17	20/23	31/21	3/2	8/6	4/19	16/16
22/20	18/33	11/0	10/3	9/13	29/2	19/14
49/1	5/5	8/4	2/19	27/3	30/9	15/26
2/7	14/4	12/8	6/23	18/20	29/11	32/17
12/5	7/12	13/15	36/1	43/3	40/8	6/2
5/20	19/8	2/34	39/6	7/40	3/4	14/2
2/24	32/3	6/38	3/50	1/5	1/14	20/4

Answer 88
7. In each box, top left x bottom right = bottom left and top right. The products are a two-digit number reading up.

Answer 89
3. Reverse the second line and subtract it from the top line to get the bottom line. 43390 – 25587 = 17803.

Answer 90
20. In each shape, the values are of the coloured squares. In column 1, they are worth 2; in column 2, they are worth 4; in column 3, they are worth 6 and in column 4, they are worth 8. The values are added together and the total goes at the bottom.

Answer 91
Blue hexagon = 2
White hexagon = 4
Shaded hexagon = 7

Answer 92

8	8	7	6	2	5	5	4	5	4	4	7	0	0	1
1	2	3	1	3	5	0	1	5	7	6	1	2	0	8
6	9	2	5	2	8	1	8	0	2	7	9	5	3	9
8	7	0	9	1	7	2	9	3	5	3	8	9	2	0
1	0	2	6	0	3	9	1	6	7	0	7	1	7	6
9	8	1	5	9	9	5	6	5	0	3	2	9	0	0
3	0	7	2	9	1	8	0	7	7	8	0	7	6	9
7	8	5	3	2	6	0	8	9	2	9	9	1	2	0
2	9	1	7	0	7	7	1	9	7	8	3	0	0	9
1	0	3	2	5	0	5	2	5	1	6	7	2	8	9
6	2	9	0	9	6	0	9	1	3	8	5	0	7	9
9	0	9	8	5	0	3	2	9	1	0	9	9	1	0

Answer 93
20.
Long bar = 8
Short bar = 2

Answer 94
121. Each block has a value according to its position in the grid. The blocks are numbered from 1 to 84, starting at the top right, and working right to left, left to right, right to left, etc. The coloured blocks in each column are then added together.

Answer 95
39. Each diamond contains three numbers. To get the bottom number, multiply the left by the middle, and add the product to the sum of the right and the left. (5 x 6) + 5 + 4 = 39.

Answer 96
D. The two sections of each shape fit together to form a magic square. Each row of the other three add to 16, but each row of D adds to 19.

Answer 97
The route is:

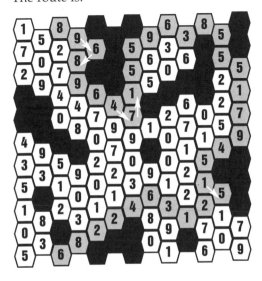

Answer 98
8. In each box the top two dishes expressed as numbers are multiplied to give the middle two dishes. The middle two dishes are then multiplied in the same way to give the bottom two.
6 x 4 = 24; 2 x 4 = 8.

Answer 99
2. Each row adds to 40.

Answer 100
23. The shapes have the following values:

7   9   5   2

Answer 101

4. The sums are
124356 x 2 = 248712
248712 x 3 = 746136
746136 x 4 = 2984544
The shapes have the values above right:

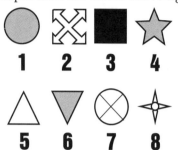

1   2   3   4

5   6   7   8

Answer 102

E. Label each row of cells from the left, and do the following multiplications:
b x k = fg; c x j = eh; a x l = di.

Answer 103

180 revolutions. (45 revolutions x 24 teeth of big wheel [1080 movements]) ÷ 6 (teeth of small wheel) = 180.

Answer 104

1. The sum of the four smallest values equals the largest value. The largest value rotates by one turn clockwise each star.

Answer 105

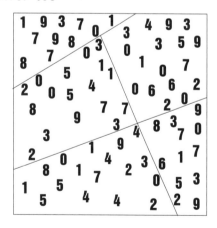

Answer 106

A. The thinnest shape to cover an area always has the greatest perimeter.

Answer 107

In each box, multiply the two bottom numbers and square the product to get the two top numbers. Read the top and bottom numbers as 2-digit figures and subtract the smaller from the larger.
√81 = 9; 9 ÷ 3 = 3; 81 − 33 = 48.

Answer 108

The highest possible total is 268, using boxes F, L, M, BB, HH, OO. The sums are:
(7 x 5) [35] + 4 + 1 = 40. (6 x 5) [30] + 2 + 1 = 33.
(7 x 5) [35] + 3 + 3 = 41. (8 x 6) [48] + 1 + 0 = 49.
(9 x 5) [45] + 1 + 1 = 47. (8 x 7) [56] + 2 + 0 = 58.
40 + 33 + 41 + 49 + 47 + 58 = 268.
The lowest possible total is 87, using boxes E, H, O, DD, GG, QQ. The sums are: (3x3) [9] +2+1=12. (3x2) [6] +1+0+7. (5x2) [10] +1+0=11. (8x2) [16] +2+0=18. (7x2) [14] +2+1=17. (4x4) [16]+4+2=22.
12+7+11+18+17+22=87.

Answer 109

Answer 110

5555
22220

Answer 111

5. Use the values represented by the black spots in the puzzle, numbered as below. Multiply each top pair of values together to get the values for the bottom pair, and subtract the bottom left value from the top right value.
4 x 7 = 28; 7 – 2 = 5.

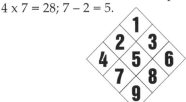

Answer 112

47. Add together all the numbers around each graph, bottom. Multiply together the three numbers around the roof, top. The answers should be the same.
5 x 2 x 12 = 120. 47 + 45 + 17 + 11 = 120.

Answer 113

5. The three smallest numbers are added together to give the largest number. The largest number is always on the right.
5 + 14 + 70 = 89.

Answer 114

Answer 115

19. Map the prime numbers from 2 to 53 into four columns.

Answer 116

32.
White ring = 3
Shaded ring = 9
Purple ring = 4

Answer 117

2 units.

Answer 118

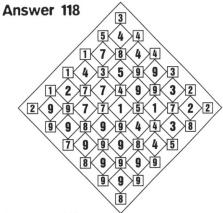

Answer 119

1009315742. The number of white boxes before the red box on each line, counting alternately from left and right.

Answer 120

E. What was external becomes internal, and vice-versa.

Answer 121

B. Count the bacteria in each Petri dish, then multiply the first number by the second number and add the third number to the product.
The 2-digit result follows. (4 x 7) + 5 = 33.

Answer 122

A = 40, B = 60. Opposite numbers are multiplied or added to get the numbers in the middle.

Answer 123

6. The numbers in the left triangles of each pair of split blocks, when multiplied together, equals the numbers in the right-hand triangles of each pair of split blocks. 7 x 8 = 56.

Answer 124

10	1	–8	39	30	21	12
2	–7	33	31	22	13	11
–6	34	32	23	14	5	3
35	26	24	15	6	4	–5
27	25	16	7	–2	–4	36
19	17	8	–1	–3	37	28
18	9	0	–9	38	29	20

Leaps of Logic

For those with a taste for remorseless logic
this section is where it all happens. Here we
tax you with everything from strange series
and mystifying matrices to cubic conundrums
and exotic enigmas. This is puzzling fun at its
most acute and is completely guaranteed to
have you biting your fingernails in frustration.

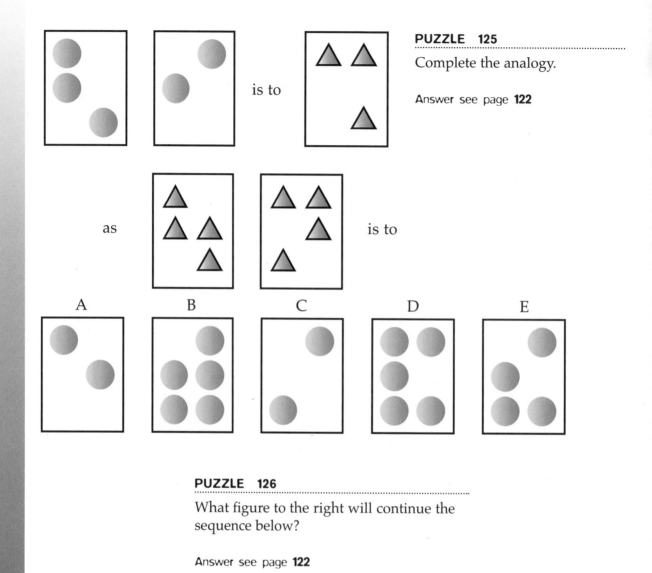

PUZZLE 125

Complete the analogy.

Answer see page **122**

PUZZLE 126

What figure to the right will continue the sequence below?

Answer see page **122**

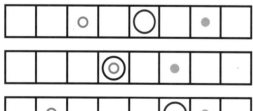

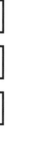

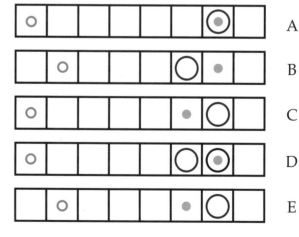

PUZZLE 127

Which of the five boxes below is most like the box above?

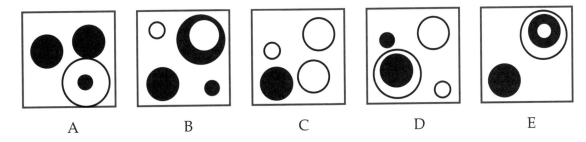

A   B   C   D   E

Answer see page **122**

PUZZLE 128

What number should replace the question mark?

Answer see page **122**

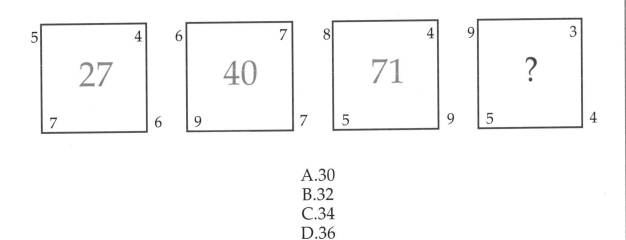

A.30
B.32
C.34
D.36
E.38

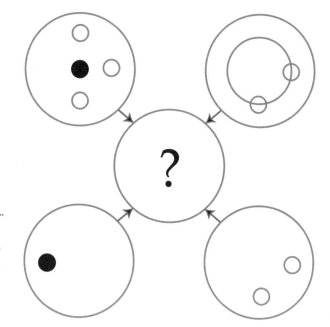

PUZZLE 129

Each line and symbol that appears in the four outer circles, above, is transferred to the middle circle according to how many times it appears, as follows:

One time — it is transferred
Two times — it is possibly transferred
Three times — it is transferred
Four times — it is not transferred

Which of the circles below should appear as the middle circle?

Answer see page 122

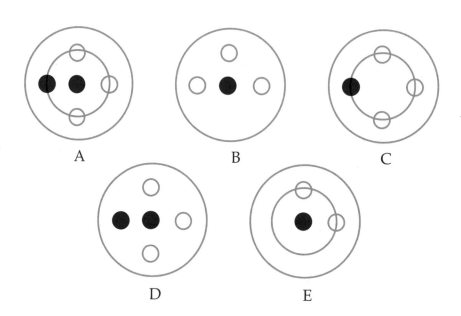

PUZZLE 130

What circle will continue the sequence and replace the question mark?

Answer see page **122**

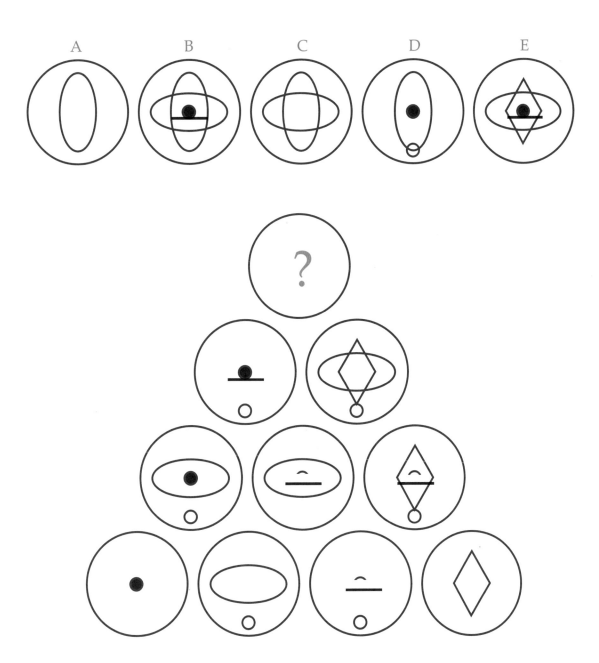

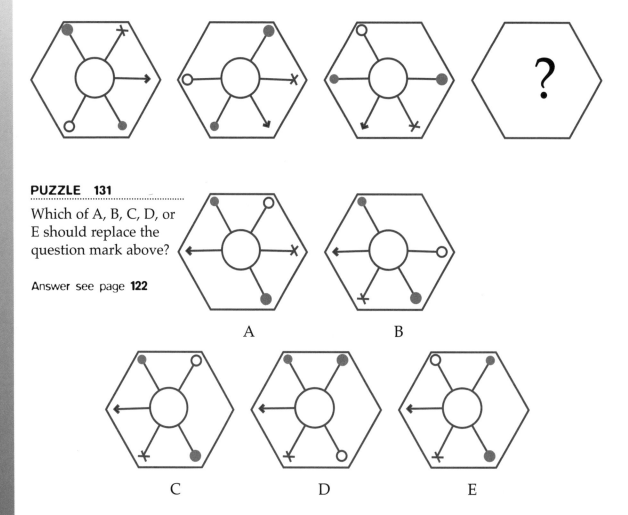

PUZZLE 131

Which of A, B, C, D, or E should replace the question mark above?

Answer see page 122

A

B

C

D

E

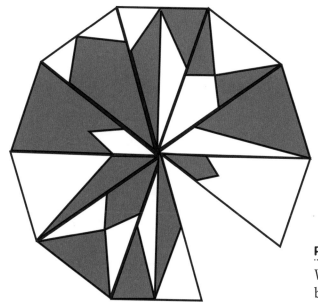

PUZZLE 132

Which of the segments below is missing from the diagram above?

Answer see page **122**

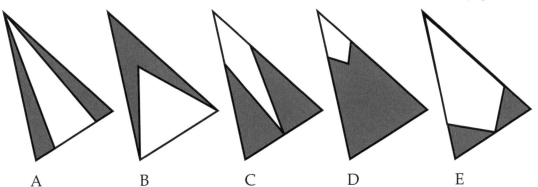

| A | B | C | D | E |

PUZZLE 133

What number will replace the question mark?

Answer see page **122**

PUZZLE 134

When the above is folded to form a cube, just one of the following can be produced. Which one is it?

Answer see page 122

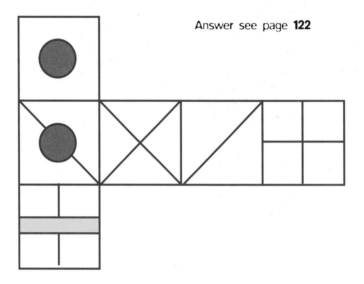

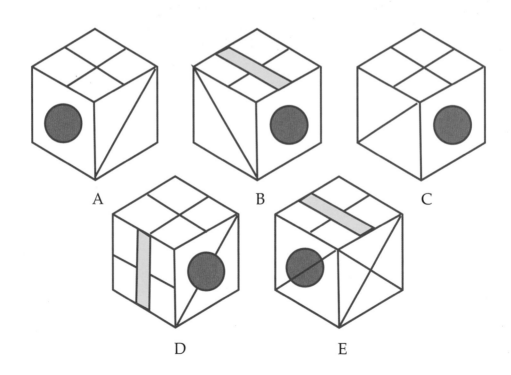

A B C

D E

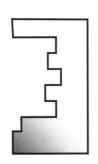

PUZZLE 135

Which piece, below, can be put with the one above to form a perfect square?

Answer see page **122**

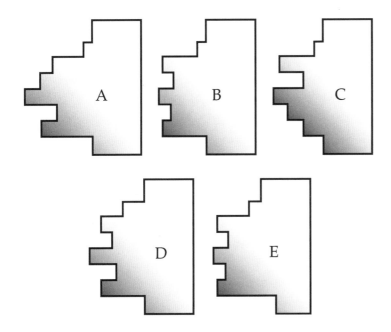

PUZZLE 136

What number should replace the question mark?

Answer see page **122**

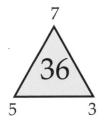
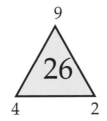
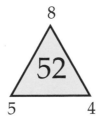
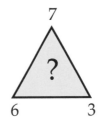

93

PUZZLE 137

Which of the following is the odd one out?

Answer see page **122**

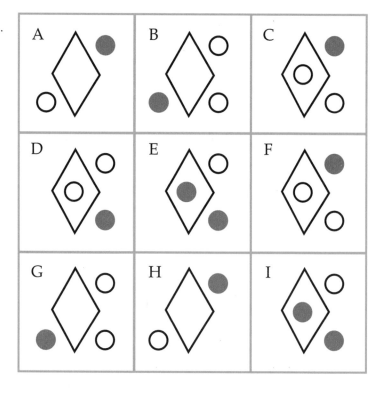

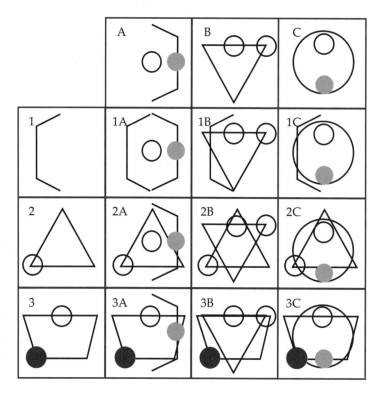

PUZZLE 138

Each of the nine squares in the grid marked 1A to 3C should incorporate all of the items which are shown in the squares of the same letter and number, at the left and top, respectively. For example, 2B should incorporate all of the symbols that are in squares 2 and B. One square, however, is incorrect. Which one is it?

Answer see page **122**

PUZZLE 139

Which of the following is the odd one out?

Answer see page **122**

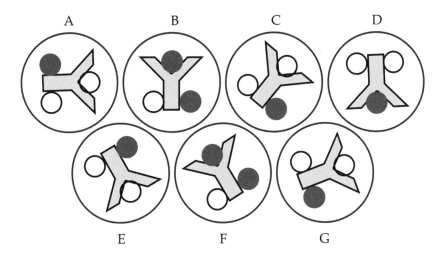

PUZZLE 140

Answer see page **122**

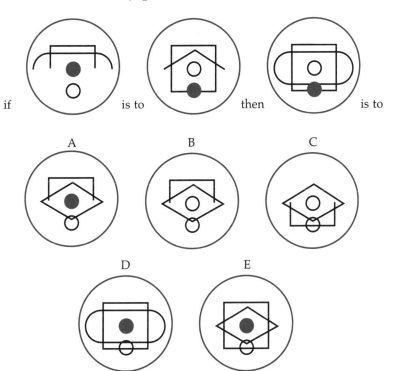

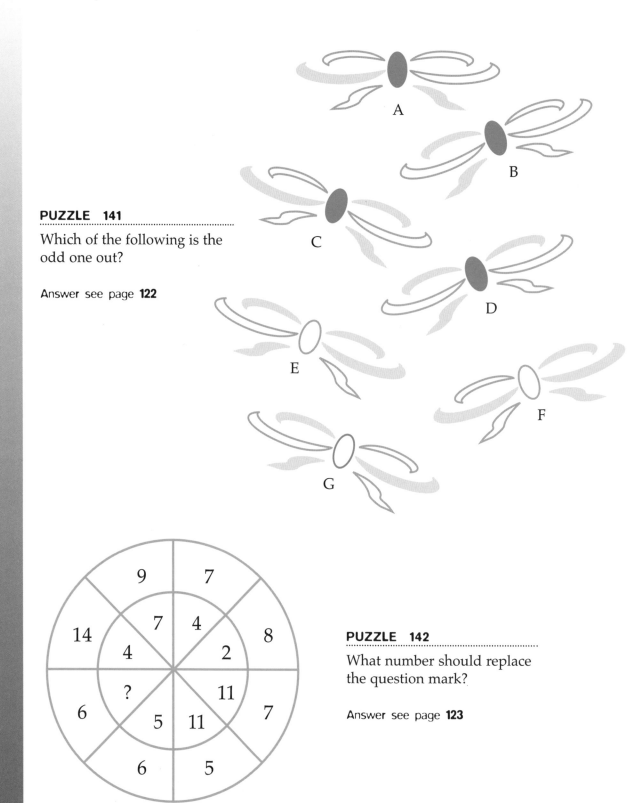

PUZZLE 141

Which of the following is the odd one out?

Answer see page **122**

PUZZLE 142

What number should replace the question mark?

Answer see page **123**

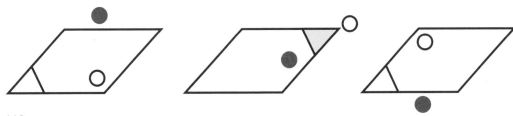

PUZZLE 143

Which of the following, below, will continue the series above?

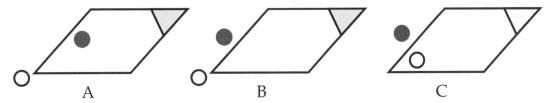

Answer see page **123**

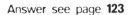

PUZZLE 144

If the missing letters in the two circles below are correctly inserted they will form antonymous words. The words do not have to be read in a clockwise direction, but the letters are consecutive. What are the words and missing letters?

Answer see page **123**

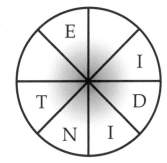

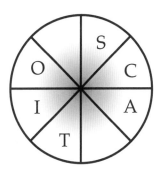

PUZZLE 145

Answer see page **123**

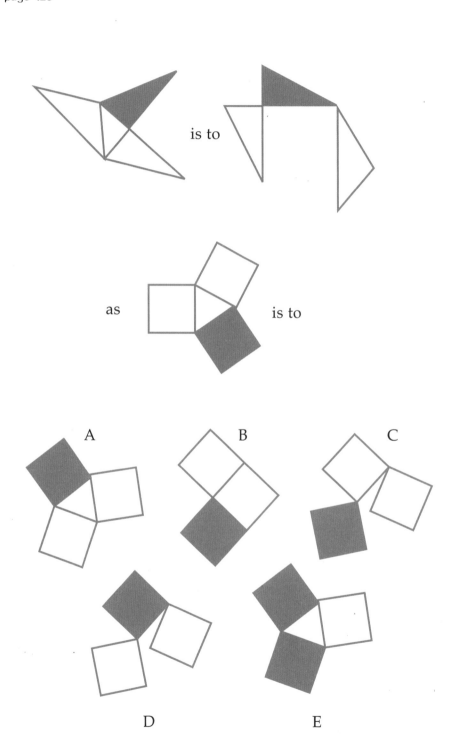

PUZZLE 146

Which of the following will replace the
question mark and complete the series?

Answer see page **123**

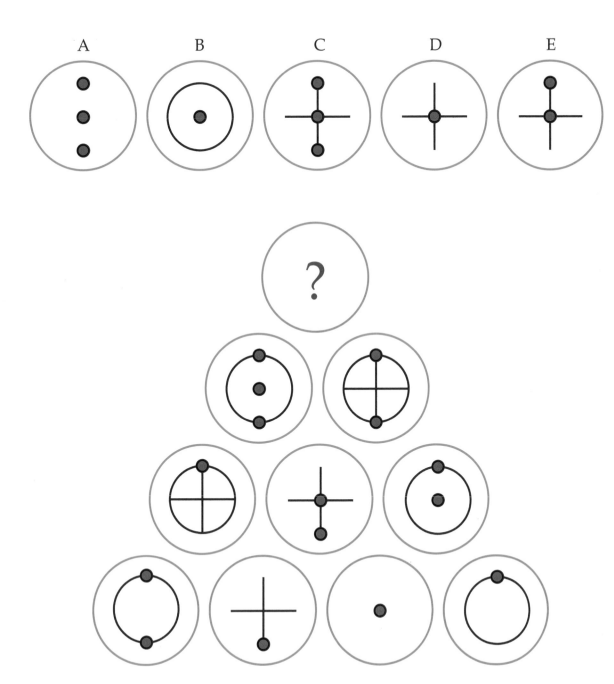

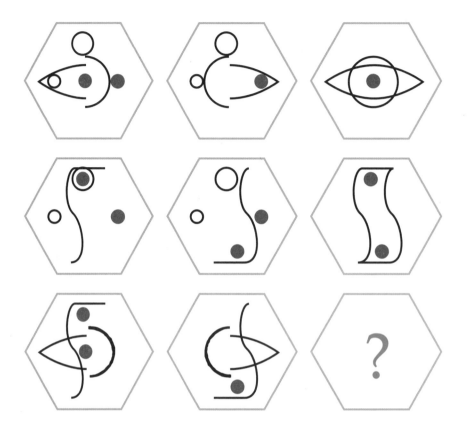

PUZZLE 147

Which of the hexagons below should
replace the question mark above?

Answer see page 123

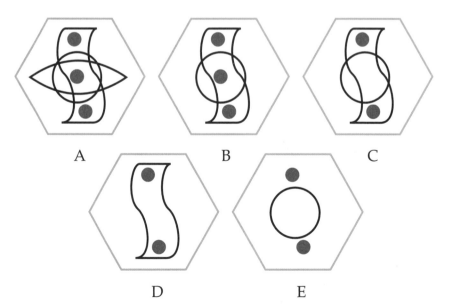

A   B   C

D   E

PUZZLE 148

Which of the circles below will continue the sequence above?

Answer see page **123**

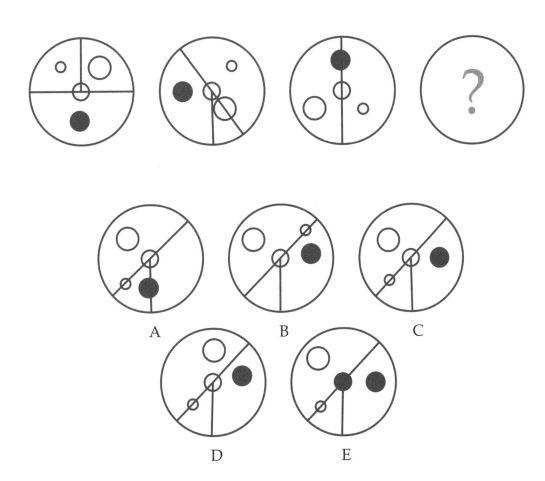

PUZZLE 149

If the missing letters in the circle (right) are correctly inserted they will form an eight-letter word. The word will not have to be read in a clockwise direction, but the letters are consecutive. What is the word and missing letters?

Answer see page **123**

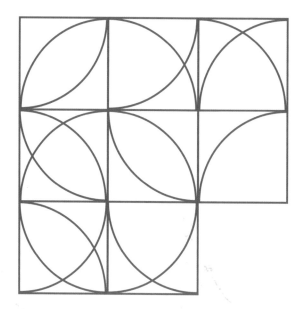

PUZZLE 150

Which of the following tiles will complete the square above?

Answer see page **123**

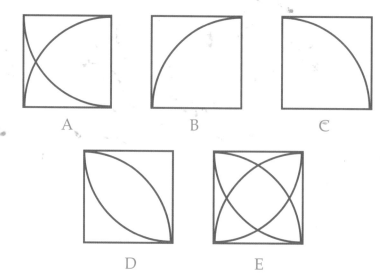

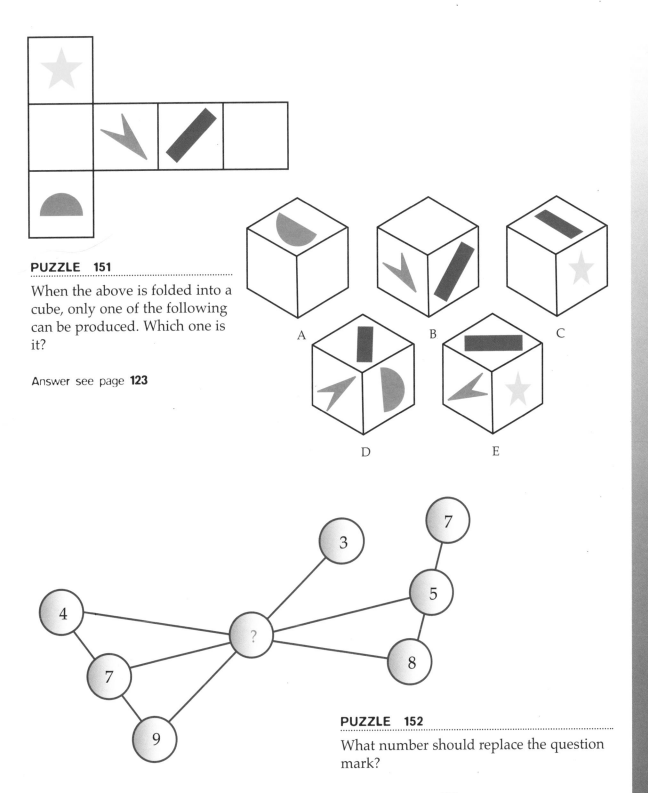

PUZZLE 151

When the above is folded into a cube, only one of the following can be produced. Which one is it?

Answer see page **123**

A   B   C

D   E

PUZZLE 152

What number should replace the question mark?

Answer see page **123**

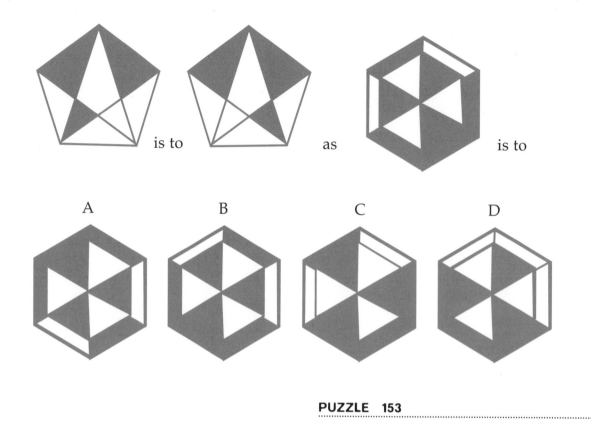

PUZZLE 153

Answer see page **123**

PUZZLE 154

What number should replace
the question mark?

Answer see page **123**

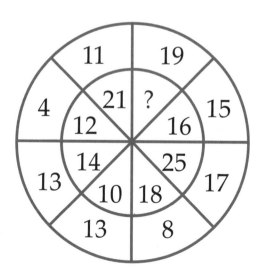

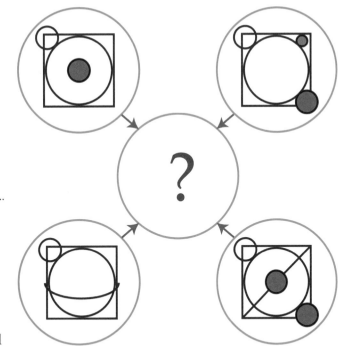

PUZZLE 155

Each line and symbol that appears in the four outer circles, above, is transferred to the middle circle according to how many times it appears, as follows:

One time — it is transferred
Two times — it is possibly transferred
Three times — it is transferred
Four times — it is not transferred

Which of the circles below should appear in the middle circle?

Answer see page **123**

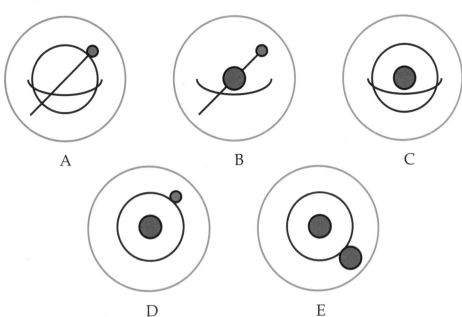

A   B   C

D   E

PUZZLE 156

What number should replace the question mark?

Answer see page **123**

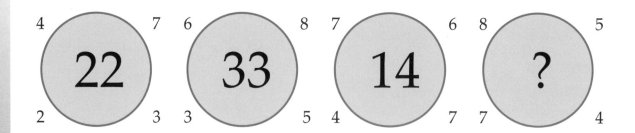

PUZZLE 157

Answer see page **123**

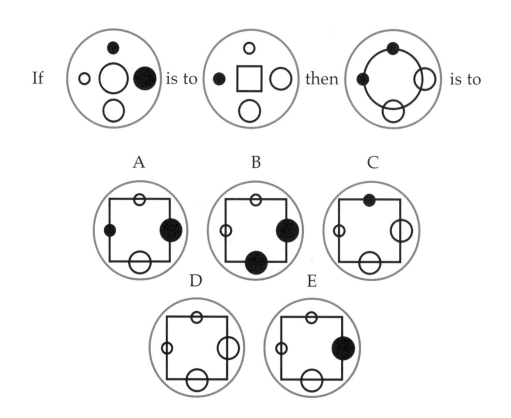

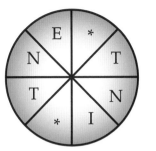 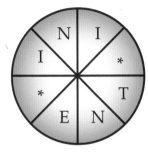

PUZZLE 158

If the missing letters in the two circles below are correctly inserted they will form synonymous words. The words do not have to be read in a clockwise direction, but the letters are consecutive. What are the words and missing letters?

Answer see page **123**

PUZZLE 159

Which of the circles at the bottom will continue the sequence above them?

Answer see page **123**

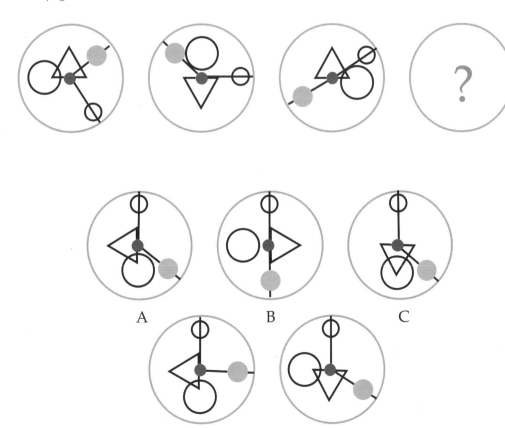

A   B   C

D   E

PUZZLE 160

Four of the five pieces below can be fitted together to form a perfect square. What piece is the odd one out?

Answer see page **124**

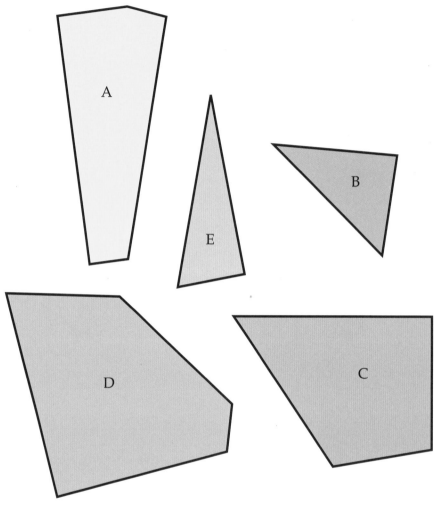

PUZZLE 161

What number should replace the question mark?

Answer see page **124**

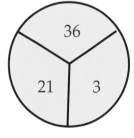
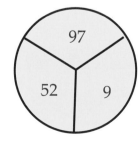
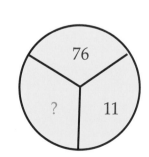

PUZZLE 162

Which shield, below, will replace the question mark above?

Answer see page **124**

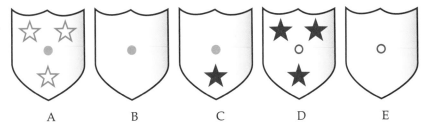

A   B   C   D   E

PUZZLE 163

Into which of the boxes A, B, C, D, or E can a dot be placed so that both dots will meet the same conditions as in the top box?

Answer see page **124**

A   B   C   D   E

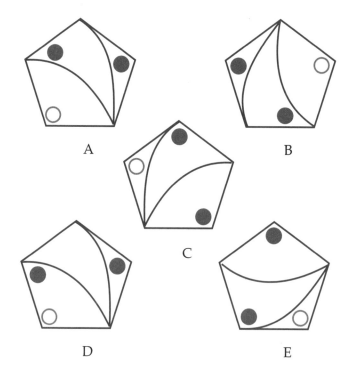

A

B

C

D

E

PUZZLE 164

Which of the following is the odd one out?

Answer see page **124**

7
6
8
2
9
3

3
9
8
6
7

7
6
8
9

?
?
?

PUZZLE 165

Which of the boxes below will follow the sequence above?

Answer see page **124**

8
7
9

A

7
9
8

B

7
8
9

C

9
7
8

D

9
8
7

E

PUZZLE 166

Each of the nine squares in the grid marked 1A to 3C should incorporate all of the items which are shown in the squares of the same letter and number, at the left and top, respectively. For example, 2B should incorporate all of the symbols that are in squares 2 and B. One square, however, is incorrect. Which one is it?

Answer see page **124**

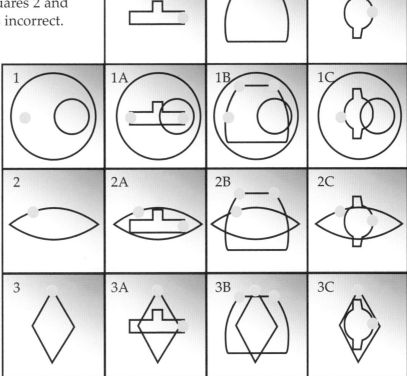

PUZZLE 167

What number should replace the question mark?

Answer see page **124**

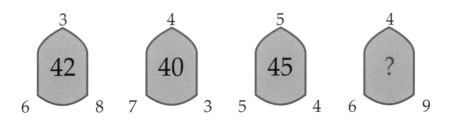

PUZZLE 168

Which of the following is the odd one out?

Answer see page **124**

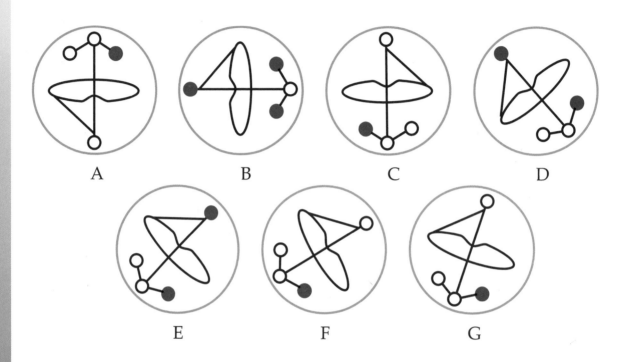

PUZZLE 169

If the missing letters in the two circles (right) are correctly inserted they will form synonymous words. The words do not have to be read in a clockwise direction, but the letters are consecutive. What are the words and missing letters?

Answer see page **124**

PUZZLE 170

What number should replace the question mark?

Answer see page **124**

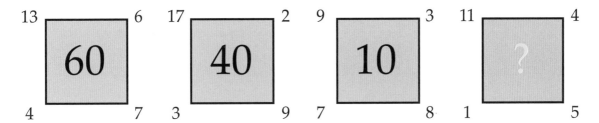

PUZZLE 171

Which of the circles A, B, C, D, or E should replace the question mark below?

Answer see page **124**

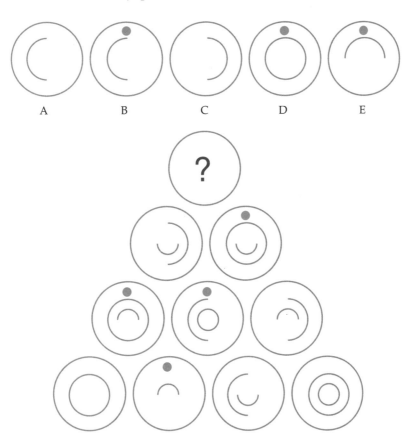

PUZZLE 172

What comes next in this sequence?

Answer see page **124**

A   B   C   D   E

A		P
R	T	O
N	I	L
I	S	

PUZZLE 173

Find the starting point and move from square to adjoining square, horizontally or vertically, but not diagonally, to spell a 12-letter word, using each letter once only. What is the missing word?

Answer see page **124**

MENSA MENSA MENSA MENSA MENSA MENSA MENSA MENSA

PUZZLE 174

Which of the following is
the odd one out?

Answer see page **124**

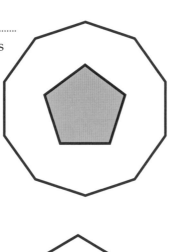

A

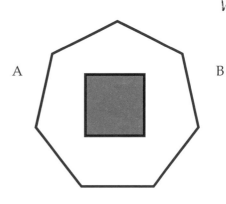

B

C

D

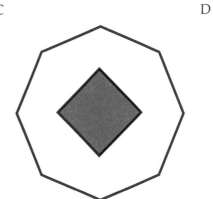

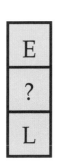

PUZZLE 175

What letter should replace the question
mark?

Answer see page **124**

PUZZLE 176

What number should replace
the question mark?

Answer see page **124**

	72	
46	16	51
	34	

	96	
38	18	43
	12	

	28	
14	?	16
	11	

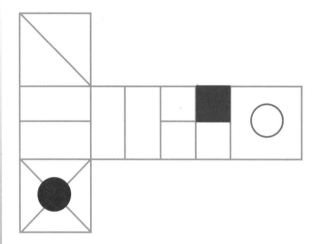

PUZZLE 177

When the above is folded to form a cube, just one of the following below can be produced. Which one is it?

Answer see page **125**

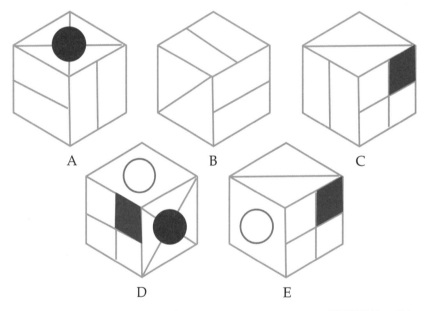

A   B   C

D   E

PUZZLE 178

What number should replace the question mark?

Answer see page **125**

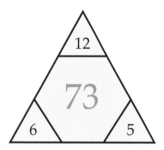

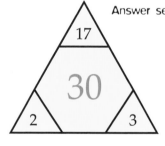

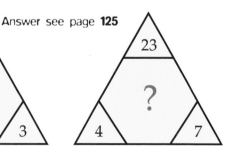

PUZZLE 179

Which of the hexagons at the bottom, A, B, C, D, or E, should replace the question mark below?

Answer see page **125**

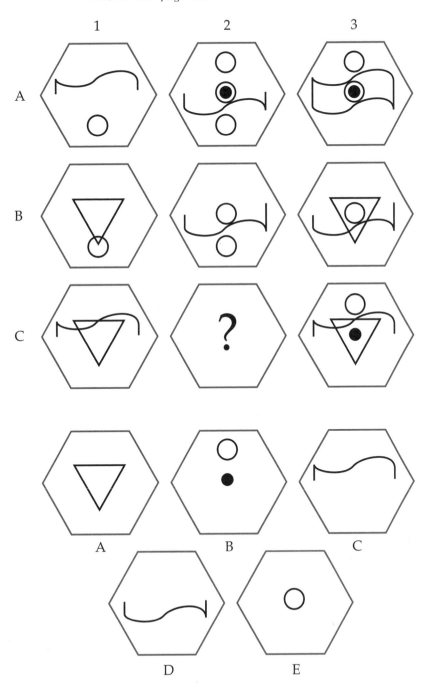

PUZZLE 180

What number should replace the question mark?

Answer see page **125**

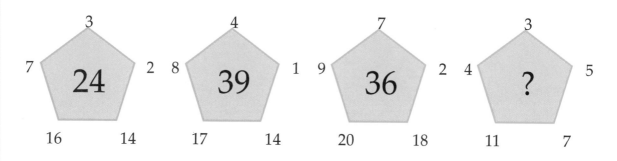

PUZZLE 181

Which of the following is the odd one out?

Answer see page **125**

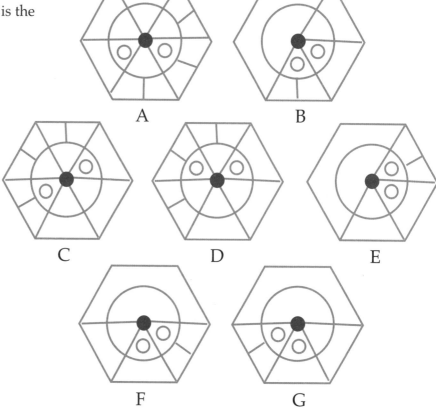

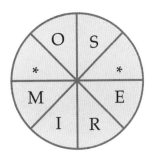 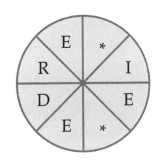

PUZZLE 182

If the missing letters in the two circles are correctly inserted they will form synonymous words. The words do not have to be read in a clockwise direction, but the letters are consecutive. What are the words and missing letters?

Answer see page **125**

PUZZLE 183

Which of the circles below should replace the question mark below?

Answer see page **125**

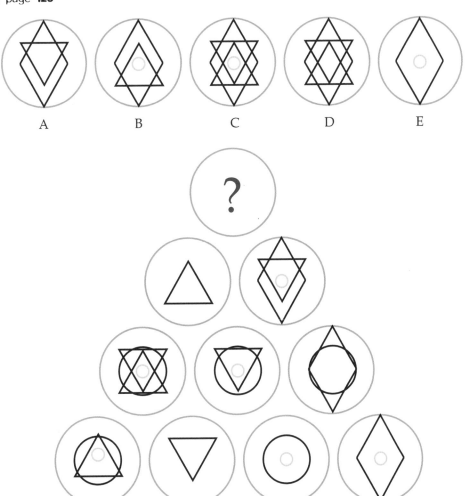

Leaps of Logic

Answers

Answer 125
E.
No figure in the same position in both rectangles is carried forward and figures change from triangle to circle and vice versa.

Answer 126
A.
There are three sequences, all alternate: the small red circle moves one forward and two back; the large blue circle moves one back and two forward; the small green spot moves one back and two forward.

Answer 127
E.
There are four circles, two black (medium-sized) and two white (one large, one small).

Answer 128
C (34).
The sums are (top left x bottom right) – (bottom left – top right) = middle.
(9 x 4) [36] – (5 – 3) [2] = 34.

The others are
(5 x 6) [30] – (7 – 4) [3] = 27;
(6 x 7) [42] – (9 – 7) [2] = 40;
(8 x 9) [72] – (5 – 4) [1] = 71.

Answer 129
A.

Answer 130
E.
Different symbols in adjoining circles on the same row are carried into the circle between them in the row above. Similar symbols in the same place are dropped.

Answer 131
C.
Every item rotates 60° clockwise each time.

Answer 132
E.
Opposite segments are mirror images except that green and white shading is reversed.

Answer 133
9.
(Top+Right) - (Bottom+Left) = Middle.

(73+3) - (39+28) = 76 - 67 = 9

Others are:

(72+55) - (83+37) = 127 - 120 = 7
and
(19+13) - (25+4) = 32 - 29 = 3

Answer 134
D.

Answer 135
B.

Answer 136
39.
The sums are (top + left) x right = middle. (7 + 6) [13] x 3 = 39.
Others are:
(7 + 5) [12] x 3 = 36;
(9 + 4) [13] x 2 = 26;
(8 + 5) [13] x 4 = 52.

Answer 137
D.
The others all have identical pairs: A and H, B and G, C and F, and E and I.

Answer 138
3A.

Answer 139
D.
The others all have identical pairs: A and E, B and F, and C and G.

Answer 140
A. The blue and white dots change position; the full square becomes a half-square and vice versa; and the oval becomes a diamond and vice versa (remaining a half-shape where appropriate).

Answer 141
D.
The others all have identical pairs:
A and E, B and F, and C and G, except that pink and white shading is reversed.

Answer 142
4. The sum of diagonally opposite segments are the same. 6 + 4 = 8 + 2.

Answer 143
A.
At each stage, the blue circle rotates 90° clockwise and goes in and out of the parallelogram; the white circle rotates 90° anti-(counter) clockwise and also goes in and out of the parallelogram; the triangle rotates 180° and changes from yellow to white and vice versa.

Answer 144
Intrepid, cautious.
The missing letters are: R and P (intrepid) and U twice (cautious).

Answer 145
C.
The left part transfers across to lie touching the original, uppermost right side.

Answer 146
D.
Different symbols in adjoining circles on the same row are carried into the circle between them in the row above. Similar symbols in the same place are dropped.

Answer 147
A.
Reading across rows and down columns, unique elements in the first two are transferred to the third (bottom or right). Common elements disappear.

Answer 148
C. At each stage, the long line rotates 45° clockwise, the short line rotates 180° and all the circles rotate 90° clockwise.

Answer 149
Hipflask.
The missing letters are F and K.

Answer 150
C.
Reading across columns and down rows, unique elements in the first two are transferred to the third (bottom or right). Common elements disappear.

Answer 151
A.

Answer 152
8.
The sum of each row of three digits is 20.

Answer 153
B. The two figures are mirror images of each other.

Answer 154
16.
The sum of inner and diagonally opposite outer segments totals 29.

Answer 155
B.

Answer 156
12.
In each case (top left x top right) – (bottom left x bottom right) = middle. (8 x 5) [40] – (7 x 4) [28] = 12.
The others are:
(7 x 4) [28] – (2 x 3) [6] = 22;
(6 x 8) [48] – (3 x 5) [15] = 33;
(7 x 6) [42] – (4 x 7) [28] = 14.

Answer 157
E.
The large circle becomes a square; a black circle on the top becomes white; and black and white swap left to right.

Answer 158
Ointment and liniment.
The missing letters are: O and M (ointment) and L and M (liniment).

Answer 159
C.
At each stage, the triangle rotates 180°, the large circle rotates 90° clockwise, the small white circle rotates 45° anti- (counter) clockwise, and the orange circle rotates 90° anti- (counter) clockwise.

Answer 160
C.

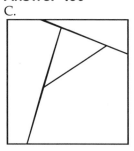

Answer 161
21. In each case (top – left) ÷ 5 = right.
(76 – 21) [55] ÷ 5 = 11.
The others are:
(36 – 21) [15] ÷ 5 = 3;
(97 – 52) [45] ÷ 5 = 9.

Answer 162
B.
Reading across columns and down rows of shields, common elements with the same shading in the first two are transferred to the third (bottom or right) and change shading. Unique elements disappear.

Answer 163
D.
One dot will appear in a enclosed small circle and another in the link between two larger circles.

Answer 164
D. The others all have identical pairs: A and B, and C and E.

Answer 165
E. The order of the column is reversed and the lowest digit is removed each time.

Answer 166
1C.

Answer 167
60.
The sums are:
(top x left) + (top x right) = middle.
(4 x 6) [24] + (4 x 9) [36] = 60.
Others are:
(3 x 6) [18] + (3 x 8) [24] = 42;
(4 x 7) [28] + (4 x 3) [12] = 40;
(5 x 5) [25] + (5 x 4) [20] = 45.

Answer 168
B. The others all have identical pairs: A and C, D and E, and F and G.

Answer 169
Impolite and insolent.
The missing letters are: M and L (impolite) and S and T (insolent).

Answer 170
30.
The sums are: (top left – bottom right) x (bottom left + top right) = middle.
(11 – 5) [6] x (1 + 4) [5] = 30.
Others are:
(13 – 7) [6] x (4 + 6) [10] = 60;
(17 – 9) [8] x (3 + 2) [5] = 40;
(9 – 8) [1] x (7 + 3) [10] = 10.

Answer 171
B. Different symbols/lines in adjoining circles on the same row are carried into the circle between them in the row above. Similar symbols/lines in the same place are dropped.

Answer 172
D.
All three shapes move down one place at each stage and the star goes from blue to white and vice versa.

Answer 173
Trampolinist. The missing letters are, reading from top to bottom: M and T.

Answer 174
B.
The number of sides of the inner figure should be half those of the outer ones. In the case of B, there is a square inside a seven-sided figure.

Answer 175
H.
Reading down each column, the letter advances three, then four places in the alphabet. Reading across, the difference is four, then five places.

Answer 176
12.
The sum of digits of the left and right numbers and also the top and bottom ones equals the middle number.
1 + 4 + 1 + 6 = 12; 2 + 8 + 1 + 1 = 12.

Answer 177
C.

Answer 178
88.
The sum is: left^2 + right^2 + top = middle.
4^2 [16] + 7^2 [49] + 23 = 88.

Others are:
6^2 [36] + 5^2 [25] + 12 = 73;
2^2 [4] + 3^2 [9] + 17 = 30.

Answer 179
B.
Reading across columns and down rows, unique elements in the first two are transferred to the third (bottom or right). Common elements disappear.

Answer 180
48.
The sums are (bottom left – bottom right) x (sum of top three numbers) = middle.
(11 – 7) [4] x (4 + 3 + 5) [12] = 48.
Others are:
(16 – 14) [2] x (7 + 3 + 2) [12] = 24;
(17 – 14) [3] x (8 + 4 + 1) [13] = 39;
(20 – 18) [2] x (4 + 3 + 5) [12] = 36.

Answer 181
C.
The others all have identical pairs: A and D, B and G, and E and F.

Answer 182
Imposter and deceiver.
The missing letters are P and T (imposter) and C and V (deceiver).

Answer 183
C.
Different symbols in adjoining circles on the same row are carried into the circle between them in the row above. Similar symbols in the same place are dropped.

Mind Marathon

Yet more chances to prove your perspicacity.
In this section you will need all your native
cunning to outwit some of the world's
wiliest puzzle setters. The section consists
mostly of spatial problems and it is these
that commonly cause most trouble to people
taking IQ tests. You need a certain quirky
kind of mind to unravel spatial problems
and this is the ideal time to find out
whether that's the kind of mind you've got.

PUZZLE 184

Six children have invented a card game and scoring system. It uses the cards up to 10, at face value, with aces scoring 1. In each round, the value of the card dealt is added to that child's score. Diamonds are worth double the face value. If two or more children are dealt cards with the same face value in one round, they lose the value of that card instead of gaining it (diamonds still doubled). They are each dealt six cards face up as shown below:

Player	Round 1	Round 2	Round 3	Round 4	Round 5	Round 6
1	6 ♥	3 ♠	ACE ♦	9 ♣	10 ♥	4 ♠
2	10 ♠	ACE ♠	7 ♥	6 ♦	5 ♠	8 ♣
3	7 ♦	8 ♥	4 ♣	3 ♥	ACE ♣	5 ♣
4	4 ♥	9 ♦	7 ♠	5 ♦	10 ♣	3 ♦
5	8 ♠	5 ♥	6 ♠	9 ♠	2 ♠	4 ♦
6	3 ♣	2 ♣	9 ♥	7 ♣	10 ♦	8 ♦

When the scores are added up, which player:

1.   Came third?
2.   Won?
3.   Came last?
4.   Was winning after the fourth cards had been dealt?
5.   Had even scores?
6.   Had a score divisible by 3?
7.   What was the second highest score?
8   What was the sum of all of the scores?

Answers see page **214**

PUZZLE 185

What numbers should replace the symbols in this grid if only the numbers 1 to 7 can be used?

Answers see page **214**

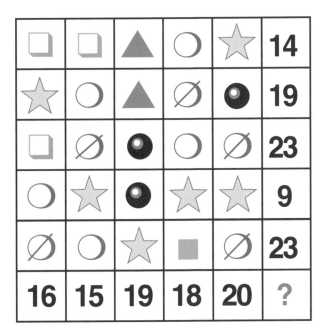

PUZZLE 186

What numbers are missing from these number grids?

Answers see page **214**

A	B	C	D	E
7	5	3	4	8
9	8	8	8	8
6	4	9	3	5
8	3	6	?	9

A	B	C	D	E
7	8	7	9	7
5	5	8	5	9
6	3	7	3	9
4	4	8	6	?

PUZZLE 187

What numbers should replace the question marks?

Answers see page **214**

A

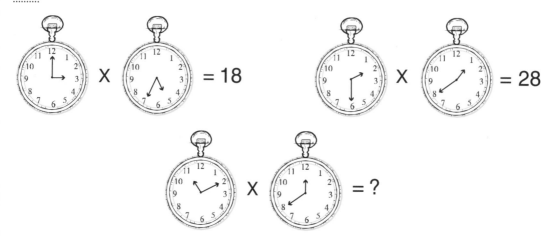

B

C
....

D
....

PUZZLE 188

What numbers should replace the question marks?

Answers see page **214**

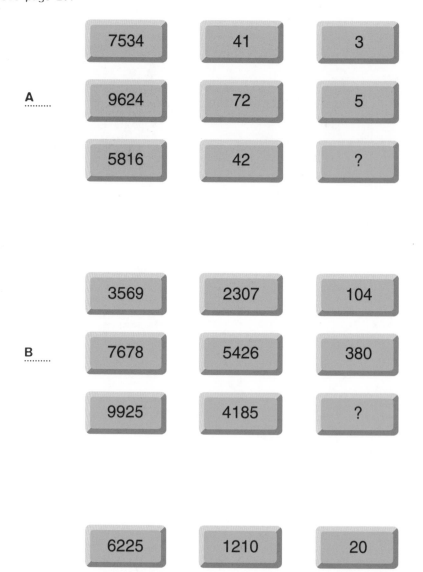

A

7534	41	3
9624	72	5
5816	42	?

B

3569	2307	104
7678	5426	380
9925	4185	?

C

6225	1210	20
7946	6324	188
3483	1224	?

PUZZLE 189

Divide these two grids into four identical shapes. The sum of the numbers contained within each of the shapes must give the totals shown.

Answers see page **214**

A

Totals 120

8	7	6	8	7	12	9	1
7	12	7	6	4	3	2	14
8	9	7	8	5	7	11	1
8	8	10	7	6	16	10	1
4	9	13	4	12	2	15	6
8	5	2	2	4	9	8	15
6	9	8	14	14	8	2	1
9	6	10	5	12	1	5	17

B

Totals 134

5	7	8	15	4	7	5	6
11	6	9	8	16	12	10	10
7	12	10	12	3	11	6	8
6	7	2	5	7	7	15	10
12	15	10	8	5	12	8	7
6	7	11	13	9	6	9	6
9	8	10	6	8	8	1	2
3	6	4	10	10	10	15	15

PUZZLE 190

The values of grids A and B are given.
What is the value of the grid C?

1

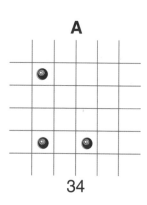

2

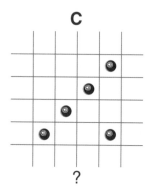

A triangle denotes the grid value and a
circle denotes twice the grid value. The
values of grids A and B are given. What is
the value of the grid C?

Answers see page **214-15**

3

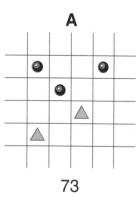

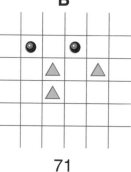

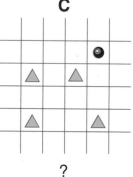

PUZZLE 191

Can you calculate the numbers missing in the figures below? Each number is used once only and is not reversed.

Answers see page **215**

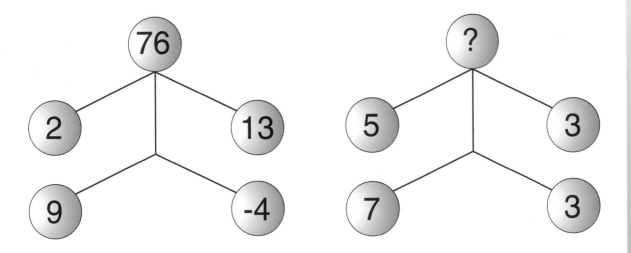

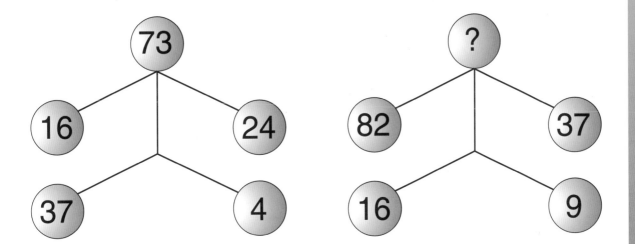

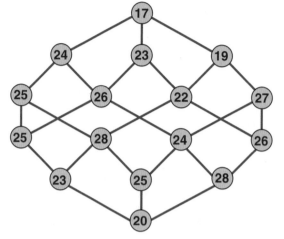

PUZZLE 192

Starting at the top number, find a route that goes down one level each time until you reach the bottom number.

1. Can you find a route where the sum of the numbers is 130?
2. Can you find two separate routes that give a total of 131?
3. What is the highest possible score and what route/s do you follow?
4. What is the lowest possible score and what route/s do you follow?

Answers see page **215**

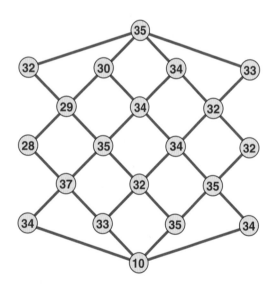

PUZZLE 193

Starting at the top number, find a route that goes down one level each time until you reach the bottom number.

1. Can you find a route where the sum of the numbers is 216?
2. Can you find two separate routes that give a total of 204?
3. What is the highest possible score and what route/s do you follow?
4. What is the lowest possible score and what route/s do you follow?
5. How many ways are there to score 211 and what route/s do you follow?

Answers see page **215**

PUZZLE 194

What is the value of the last string in each of these problems if the first three strings have values as given? Green, white and shaded circles have different values.

Answers see page **215**

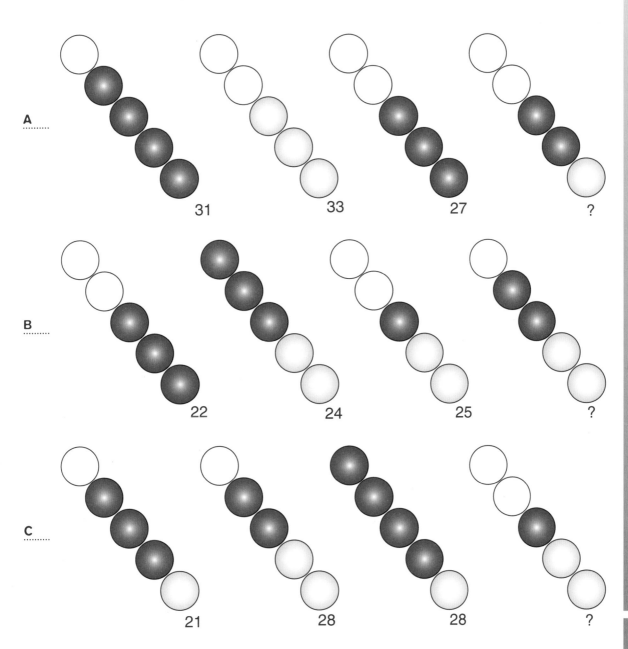

A

31   33   27   ?

B

22   24   25   ?

C

21   28   28   ?

137

PUZZLE 195 Example

The numbers on the grids below are found by giving the value of any symbol that is adjacent horizontally, vertically or diagonally. The numbers are then halved in adjacent boxes. If there is more than one value that can go in a box, then they are added together. See examples below.

	A	B	C	D	E	F
1	2	2	2	2	0	0
2	4	4	4	2	0	0
3	4	×	4	2	0	0
4	4	4	4	2	0	0
5	2	2	2	2	0	0
6	0	0	0	0	0	0

	A	B	C	D	E	F
1	0	5	5	5	5	5
2	0	5	10	10	10	5
3	0	5	10	△	10	5
4	0	5	10	10	10	5
5	0	5	5	5	5	5
6	0	0	0	0	0	0

	A	B	C	D	E	F
1	2	7	7	7	5	5
2	4	9	14	12	10	5
3	4	×	14	△	10	5
4	4	9	14	12	10	5
5	2	7	7	7	5	5
6	0	0	0	0	0	0

If $\times = 4$ & $\triangle = 10$

The grid value would look like the example

$$C1 = (D3 \times \tfrac{1}{2}) + (B3 \times \tfrac{1}{2}) = 7$$
$$A5 = B3 \times \tfrac{1}{2} = 2$$
$$D4 = D3 + (B3 \times \tfrac{1}{2}) = 12$$

PUZZLE 195

From the information in the grid opposite, complete the grid and answer the questions that follow:

	A	B	C	D	E	F
1						
2	32	●			T	16
3			□			
4		T			□	
5					●	
6			22			28

A.   What is the value of square D1?
B.   What is the value of square A3?
C.   What is the value of square F3?
D.   What square has the highest value?
E.   What is the value of □ ?
F.   What is the value of the lowest square?
G.   What are the values of the symbols ● and T ?
H.   Which 3 squares have a value of 32?

Answers see page **215**

PUZZLE 196

Now try this more difficult grid using the same rules:

	A	B	C	D	E	F
1	△					24
2			★	△	△	
3	37		⊗			
4					⊗	
5		⊗				
6				△		20

A.   What are the values of the three symbols?
B.   What is the value of the highest square?
C.   What is the value of square C4?
D.   What is the value of the lowest square?
E.   What is the value of square E3?
F.   How many squares have a value of 64?

Answers see page **215**

PUZZLE 197

Start at the top-left circle and move clockwise. Calculate the number that replaces the question marks in the following:

Answers see page **215**

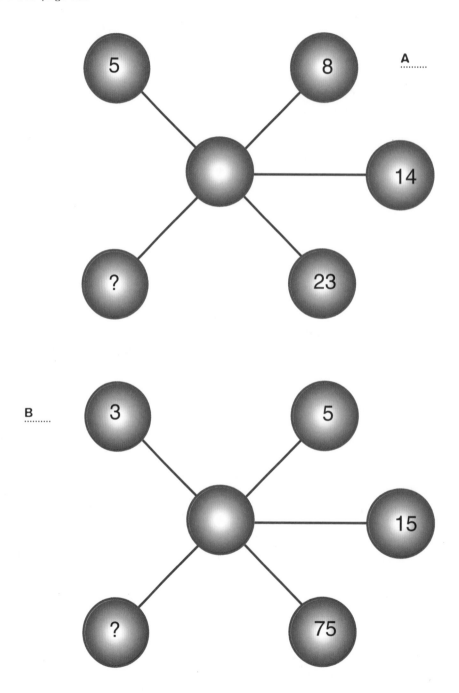

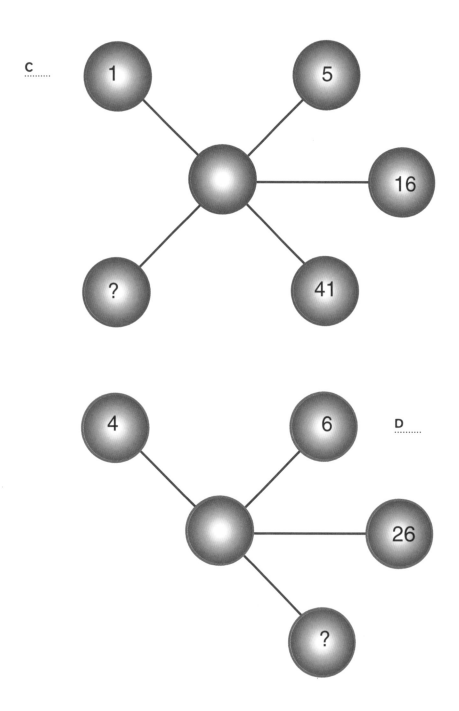

C

D

PUZZLE 198

The number in the middle knot of the following bow ties is reached by using all of the outer numbers only once. You cannot reverse the numbers to obtain the answers. Which numbers should replace the question marks?

Answers see page **215**

A

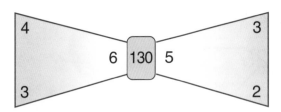
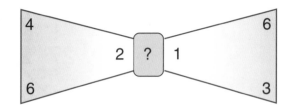

B

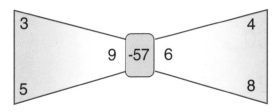
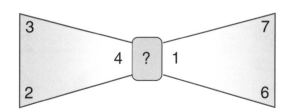

C

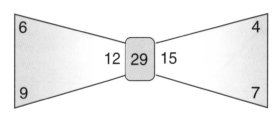
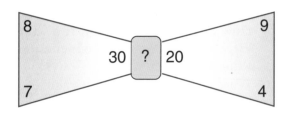

PUZZLE 199

In the grid below, the intersections have a value equal to the sum of their four touching numbers. Can you answer the questions at the bottom:

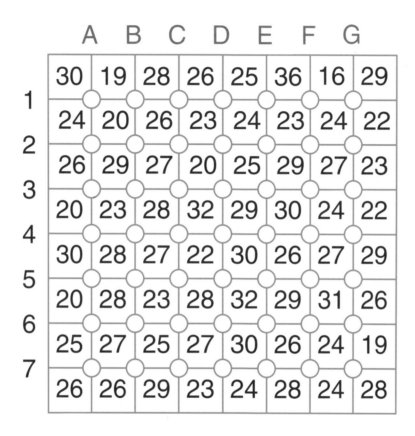

A.   What are the grid references for the three intersection points with a value of 100?
B.   Which intersection point/s has a value of 92?
C.   How many intersections have a value of less than 100?
D.   Which intersection has the highest value?
E.   Which intersection has the lowest value?
F.   Which intersection/s has a value of 115?
G.   How many intersections have a value of 105 and which are they?
H.   How many intersections have a value of 111 and which are they?

Answers see page **215**

PUZZLE 200

Can you find the missing values on the roofs of the following houses? Each of the numbers on the windows and door must be used only once and no number can be reversed.

Answers see page **216**

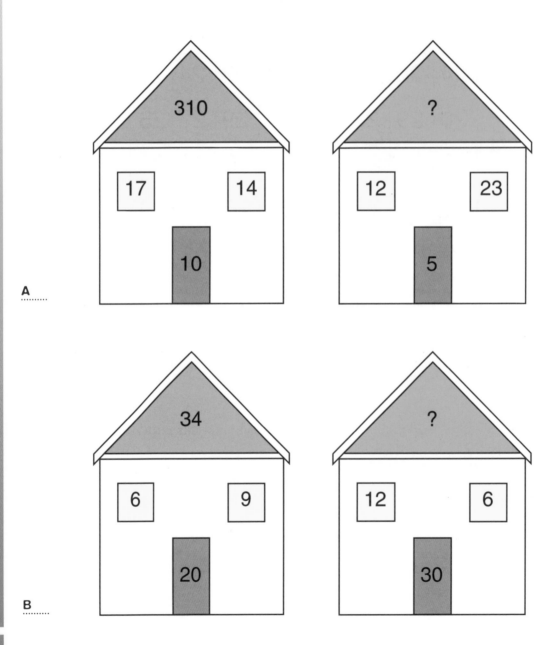

A

B

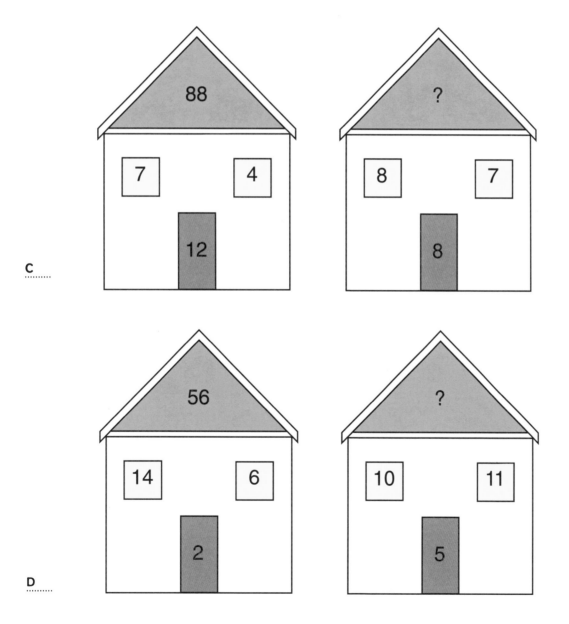

C

D

PUZZLE 201

Which of the following is the odd one out?

Answers see page **216**

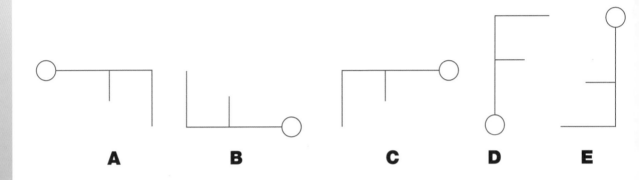

A   **B**   **C**   **D**   **E**

PUZZLE 202

Which of the following is the odd one out?

Answers see page **216**

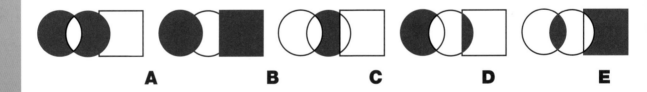

A   **B**   **C**   **D**   **E**

PUZZLE 203

Which of the following is the odd one out?

Answers see page **216**

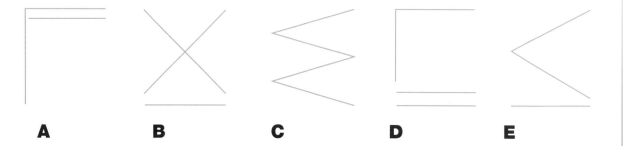

PUZZLE 204

Which of the following is the odd one out?

Answers see page **216**

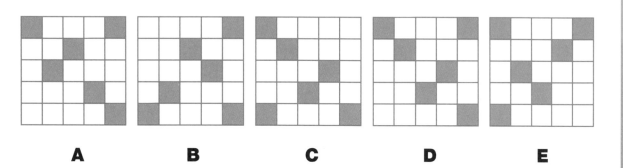

PUZZLE 205

Which of the following is the odd one out?

Answers see page **216**

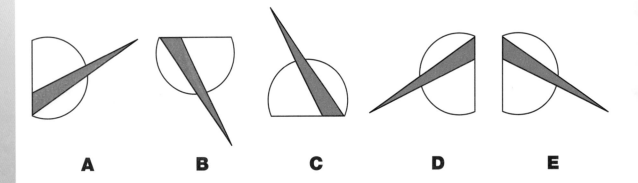

A   **B**   **C**   **D**   **E**

PUZZLE 206

Which of the following is the odd one out?

Answers see page **216**

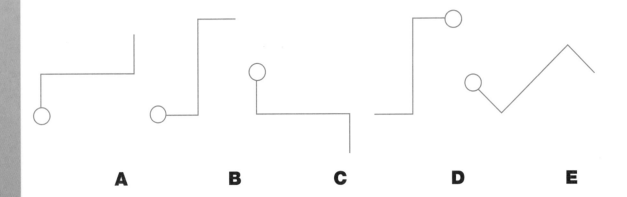

A   **B**   **C**   **D**   **E**

PUZZLE 207

Which of the following is the odd one out?

Answers see page **216**

PUZZLE 208

Which of the following is the odd one out?

Answers see page **216**

PUZZLE 209

Which of the following is the odd one out?

Answers see page **216**

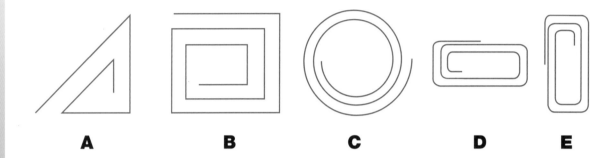

A   **B**   **C**   **D**   **E**

PUZZLE 210

Which of the following is the odd one out?

Answers see page **216**

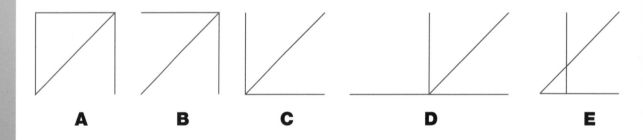

A   **B**   **C**   **D**   **E**

PUZZLE 211

Which arrangement is missing from these sequences?

Answers see page **216**

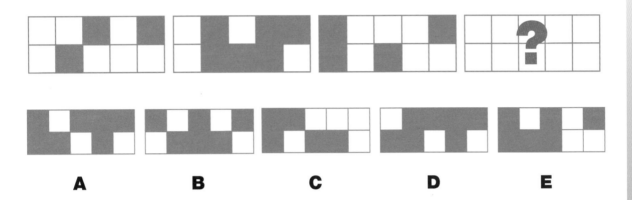

A   **B**   **C**   **D**   **E**

PUZZLE 212

Which arrangement is missing from these sequences?

Answers see page **216**

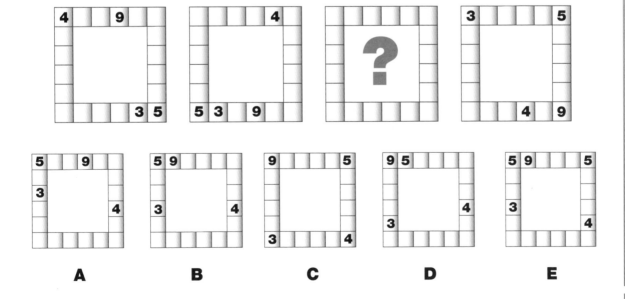

A   **B**   **C**   **D**   **E**

PUZZLE 213

Which arrangement is missing from these sequences?

Answers see page **216**

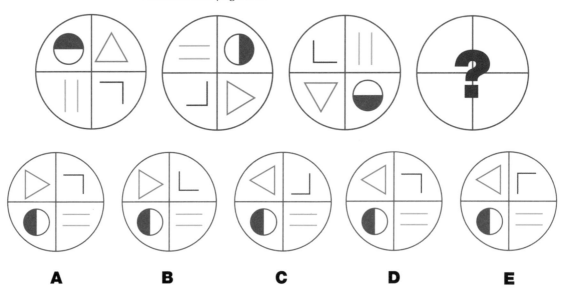

A   **B**   **C**   **D**   **E**

PUZZLE 214

Which arrangement is missing from these sequences?

Answers see page **216**

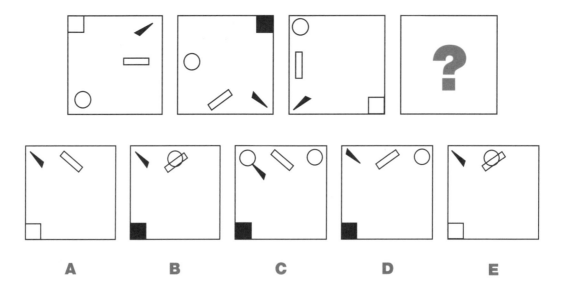

A   **B**   **C**   **D**   **E**

PUZZLE 215

Which arrangement is missing from these sequences?

Answers see page **216**

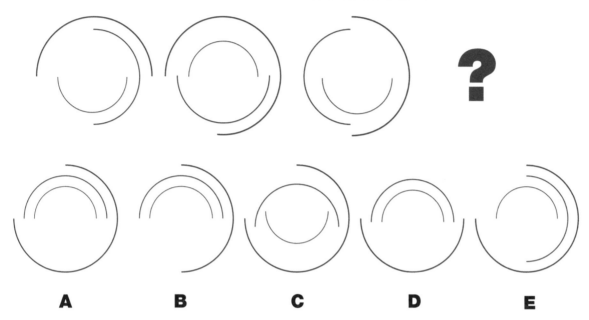

A   **B**   **C**   **D**   **E**

PUZZLE 216

Which arrangement is missing from these sequences?

Answers see page **216**

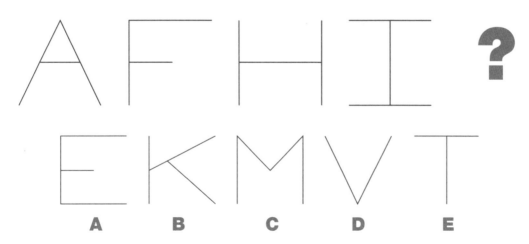

A   **B**   **C**   **D**   **E**

PUZZLE 217

Which arrangement is missing from these sequences?

Answers see page **216**

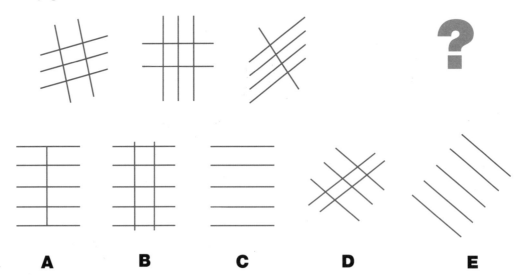

A   B   C   D   E

PUZZLE 218

Which arrangement is missing from these sequences?

Answers see page **216**

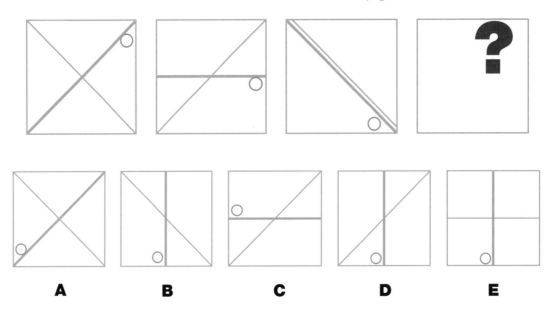

A   B   C   D   E

PUZZLE 219

Which arrangement is missing from these sequences?

Answers see page **216**

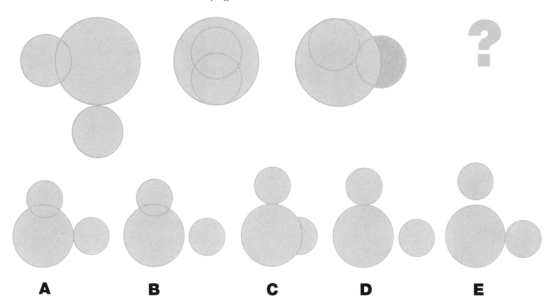

A   B   C   D   E

PUZZLE 220

Which arrangement is missing from these sequences?

Answers see page **216**

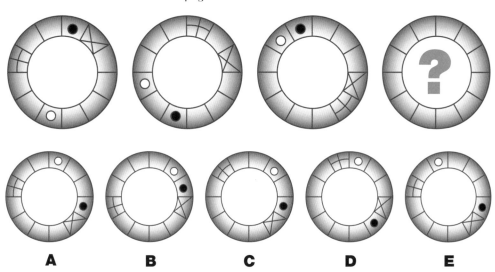

A   B   C   D   E

PUZZLE 221

Which arrangement is missing from these sequences?

Answers see page **216**

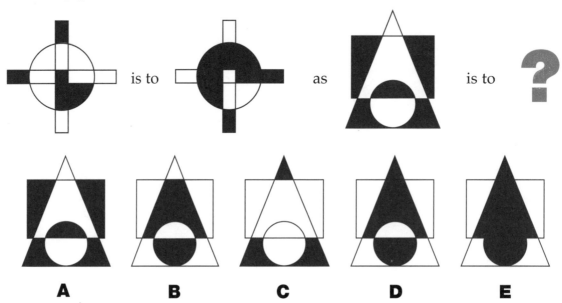

A   **B**   **C**   **D**   **E**

PUZZLE 222

Which arrangement is missing from these sequences?

Answers see page **216**

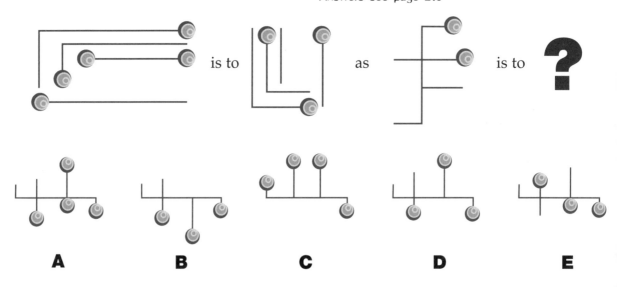

A   **B**   **C**   **D**   **E**

PUZZLE 223

Which arrangement is missing from these sequences?

Answers see page **216**

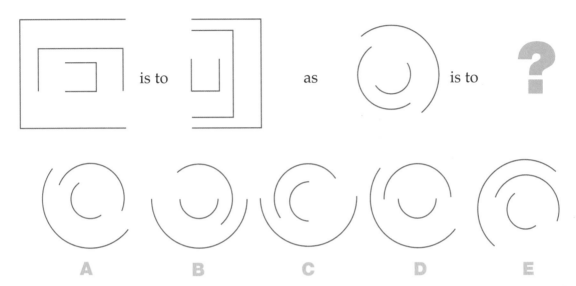

PUZZLE 224

Complete the analogy.

Answers see page **216**

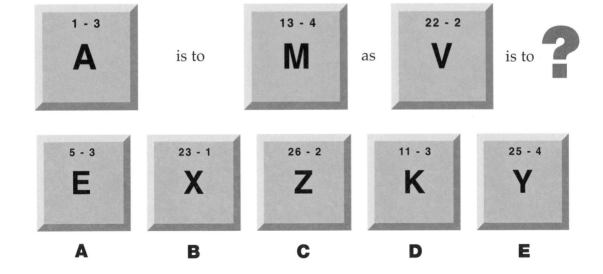

PUZZLE 225 Example

These are all mirror image problems. One of the four given images has an error on it.

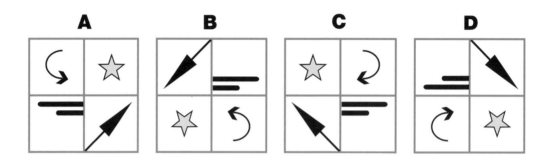

Rearranged

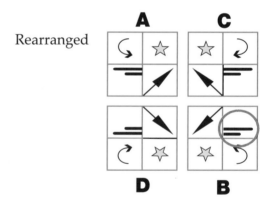

B is the odd one out as  should be

PUZZLE 225

Each one of the next four puzzles is a mirror image problem. Which of A, B, C or D is the odd one out?

Answers see page **216**

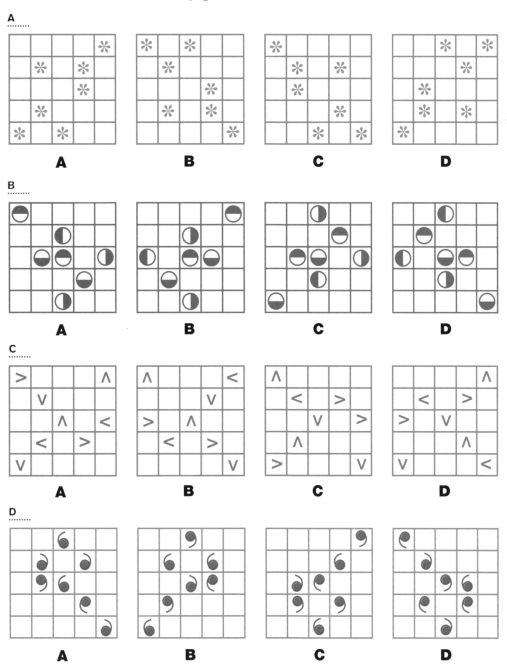

PUZZLE 226

No sign is used on more than one side of the box. Which of these is not a view of the same box?

Answers see page **217**

A
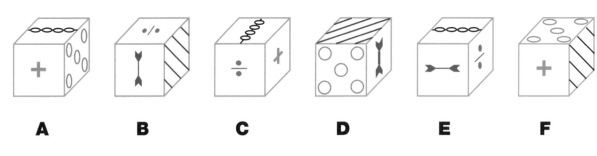

B
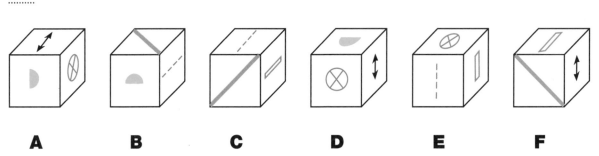

C
....

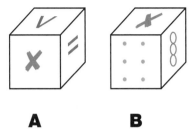

A　　　**B**　　　**C**　　　**D**　　　**E**　　　**F**

D
....

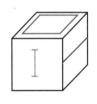

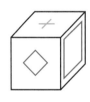

A　　　**B**　　　**C**　　　**D**　　　**E**　　　**F**

E
....

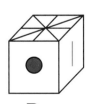

A　　　**B**　　　**C**　　　**D**　　　**E**　　　**F**

PUZZLE 227

Which of these boxes can be made from
the template?

Answers see page **217**

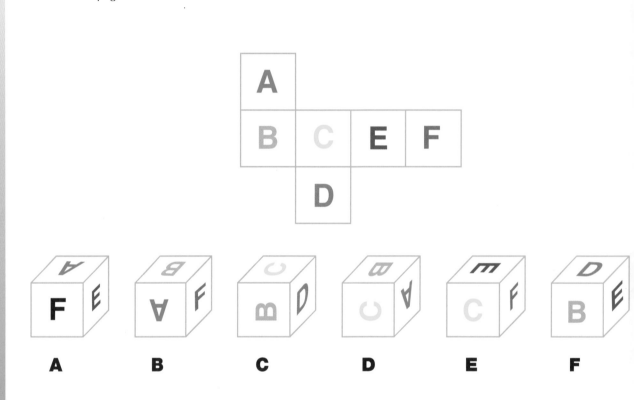

PUZZLE 228

Which of these boxes can be made from the template?

Answers see page **217**

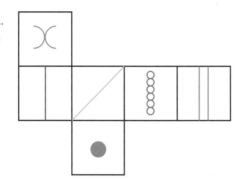

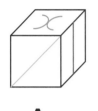
A

B

C

D

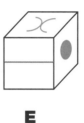
E

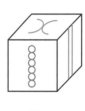
F

PUZZLE 229

Which of these boxes can be made from the template?

Answers see page **217**

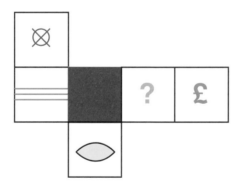

A

B

C

D

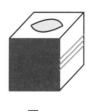
E

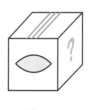
F

PUZZLE 230

Which of these boxes can be made from the template?

Answers see page **217**

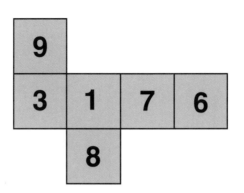

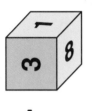
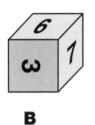

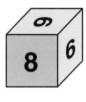
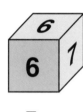

A   **B**   **C**   **D**   **E**   **F**

PUZZLE 231

Which of these boxes can be made from the template?

Answers see page **217**

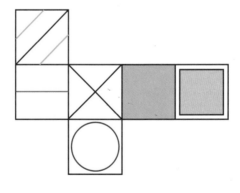

A   **B**   **C**   **D**   **E**   **F**

PUZZLE 232

Can you determine which shape has not been used in the top figure?

Answers see page **217**

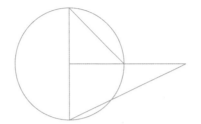

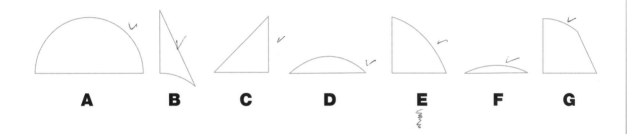

A   **B**   **C**   **D**   **E**   **F**   **G**

PUZZLE 233

Can you determine which shape has not been used in the top figure?

Answers see page **217**

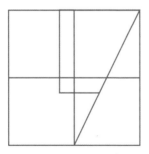

A   **B** **C** **D** **E**   **F**   **G**   **H**   **I**   **J**

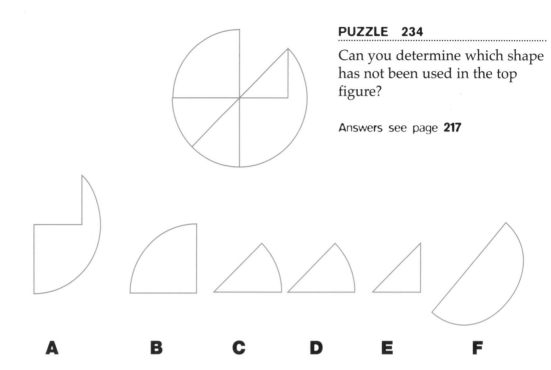

PUZZLE 234

Can you determine which shape has not been used in the top figure?

Answers see page **217**

PUZZLE 235

Which figure should replace the question mark?

Answers see page **217**

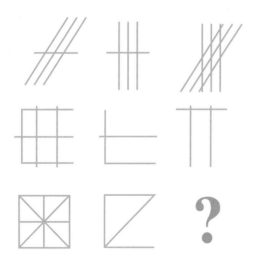

A   B   C   D   E

PUZZLE 236

Which figure should replace the question mark?

Answers see page **217**

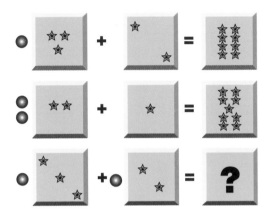

PUZZLE 237

Which of the shapes, A, B, C, D or E, cannot be made from the dots if a line is drawn through all of the dots at least once?

Answers see page **217**

A   **B**   **C**   **D**   **E**

PUZZLE 238

Which of the shapes, A, B, C, D or E, cannot be made from the dots if a line is drawn through all of the dots at least once?

Answers see page **217**

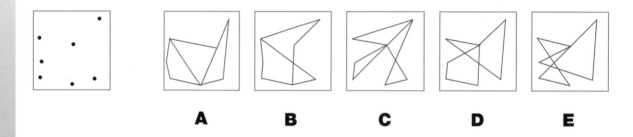

PUZZLE 239

Which of the shapes, A, B, C, D or E, cannot be made from the dots if a line is drawn through all of the dots at least once?

Answers see page **217**

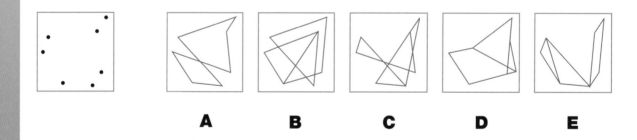

PUZZLE 240

Which of the shapes, A, B, C, D or E, cannot be made from the dots if a line is drawn through all of the dots at least once?

Answers see page **217**

A　　**B**　　**C**　　**D**　　**E**

PUZZLE 241

Which of the shapes, A, B, C, D or E, cannot be made from the dots if a line is drawn through all of the dots at least once?

Answers see page **217**

A　　**B**　　**C**　　**D**　　**E**

PUZZLE 242

The graph below shows the examination results of students taking their school leaving exams. 30 children took tests.

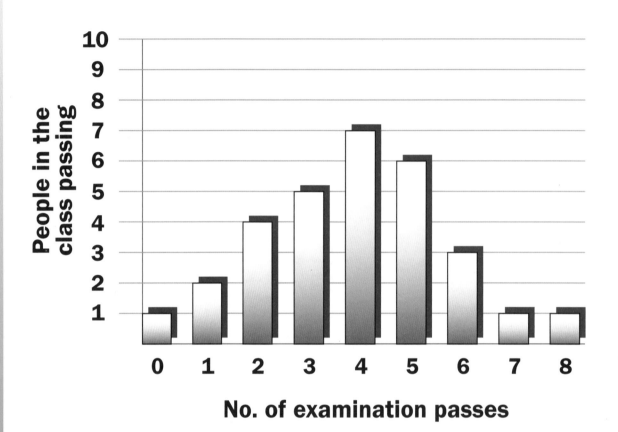

No. of examination passes

A. What was the average number of exam passes per student?
B. If the top 5 students were not in this class, what would have been the average number of exam passes per student?
C. If 10% took 8 tests, 70% took 6 tests and 20% took 4 tests, how many test papers had a fail mark?

Answers see page **217**

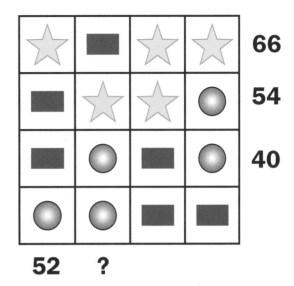

PUZZLE 243

What number should replace the question mark and what are the values of the symbols?

Answers see page **217**

PUZZLE 244

What number should replace the question mark?

Answers see page **217**

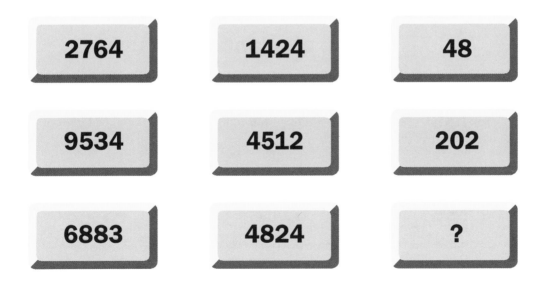

PUZZLE 245

What number should replace the question mark?

Answers see page **217**

7935	2765	1755
6188	5368	3604
9856	5488	?

PUZZLE 246

What number should replace the question mark?

Answers see page **217**

6459	5204	200
7288	5166	360
9768	7422	?

PUZZLE 247

What numbers should replace the question
marks in these boxes?

Answers see page **217**

A

A	B	C	D	E
3	1	4	7	9
7	0	2	8	6
6	5	1	4	7
2	2	3	9	?

B

A	B	C	D	E
8	2	6	3	4
5	3	4	2	3
9	1	7	3	5
7	6	8	3	?

C

A	B	C	D	E
1	5	6	2	7
4	1	5	8	9
7	3	2	6	9
6	2	?	4	?

PUZZLE 248

How many circles are missing from the boxes with the question marks?

Answers see page **217**

(2 circles)	X	(2 circles)	=	0000
(3 circles)	X	(2 circles)	=	?
(2 circles)	+	(2 circles)	=	00
(3 circles) A	−	(2 circles)	=	0

★	÷	n	=	0
2(★	X	2n)	=	0000 0 0000
2(★ ★	−	2n)	=	000
★ B	+	6n	=	?

PUZZLE 249

What numbers should replace the question marks?

Answers see page **218**

A

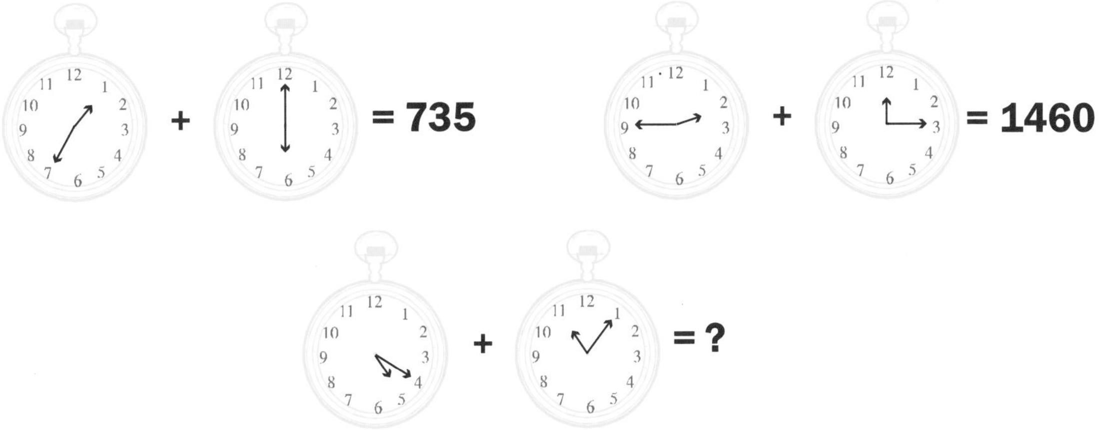

+ **= 735**   **+** **= 1460**

+ **= ?**

B

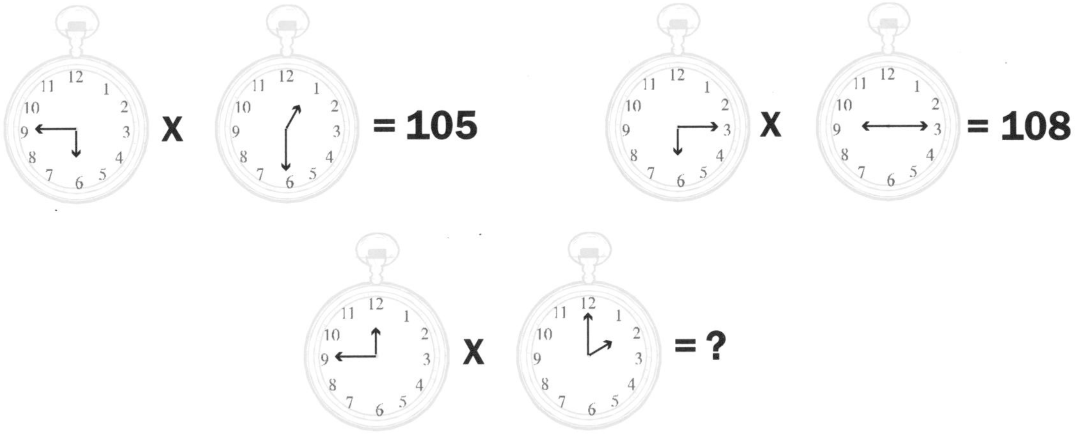

X **= 105**   **X** **= 108**

X **= ?**

PUZZLE 250

What numbers should replace the question marks?

Answers see page **218**

A

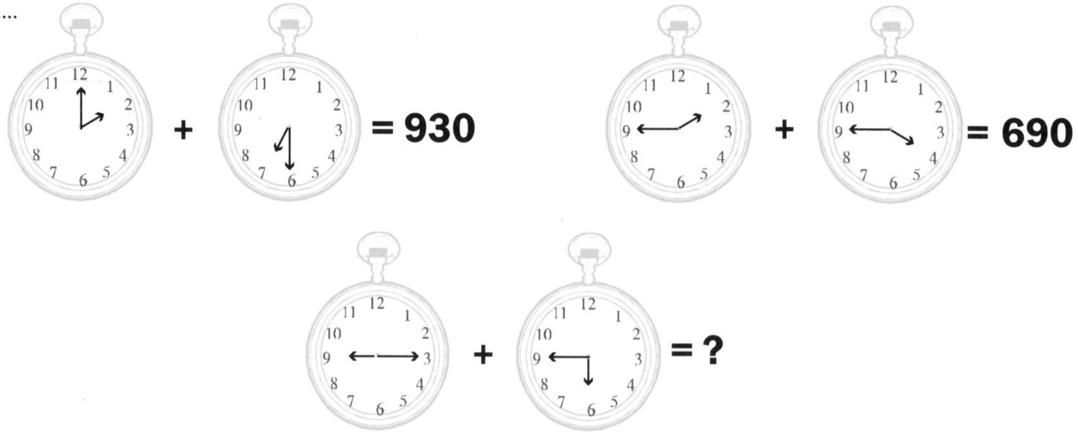

= 930

= 690

= ?

B

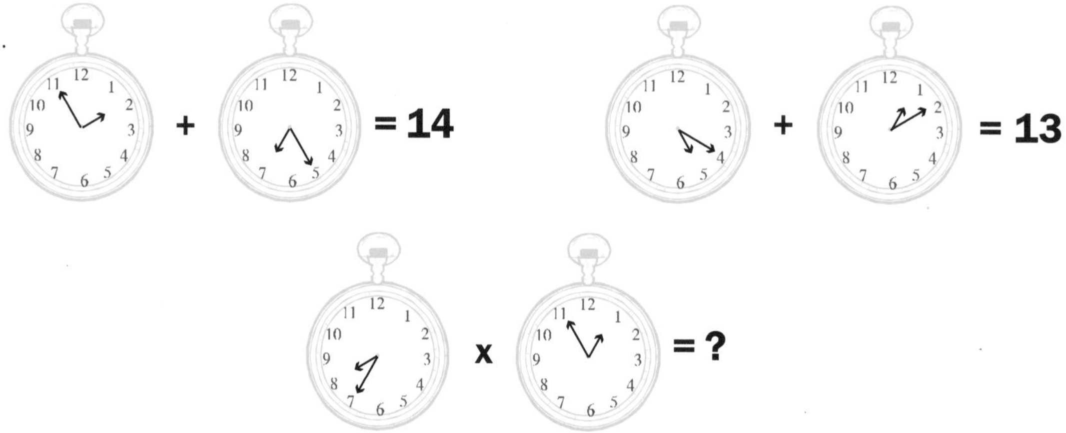

= 14

= 13

= ?

PUZZLE 251

Divide these two grids into SIX identical shapes. The sum of the numbers in each section must give the total shown.

Answers see page **218**

Total 100

18	6	4	30	47	29
45	30	6	18	17	2
1	21	1	42	23	5
3	28	7	17	1	6
44	4	32	43	30	40

Total 18

6	2	3	4	4	3
3	5	5	2	6	2
5	3	1	3	5	0
2	4	5	3	0	5
3	3	4	6	6	5

PUZZLE 252

What number should replace the question marks in these grids?

Answers see page **218**

6	4	6	5	8
2	9	8	2	1
5	0	3	4	7
3	2	1	3	1
4	7	?	4	3

3	8	7	4	5
5	9	2	6	1
3	2	5	3	7
6	9	3	7	2
1	4	?	1	8

PUZZLE 253

The numbers in the left-hand box move clockwise around the square to the positions shown in the box on the right. In which positions should the missing numbers appear?

Answers see page **218**

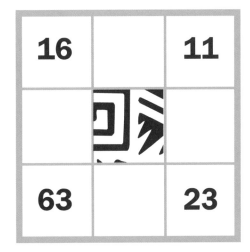

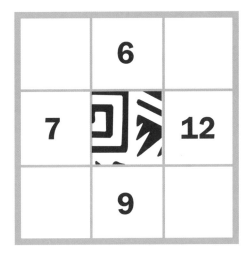

MENSA MENSA MENSA MENSA MENSA MENSA MENSA MENSA

PUZZLE 254

The values of grids A and B are given.
What is the value of each of the C grids?

Answers see page **218**

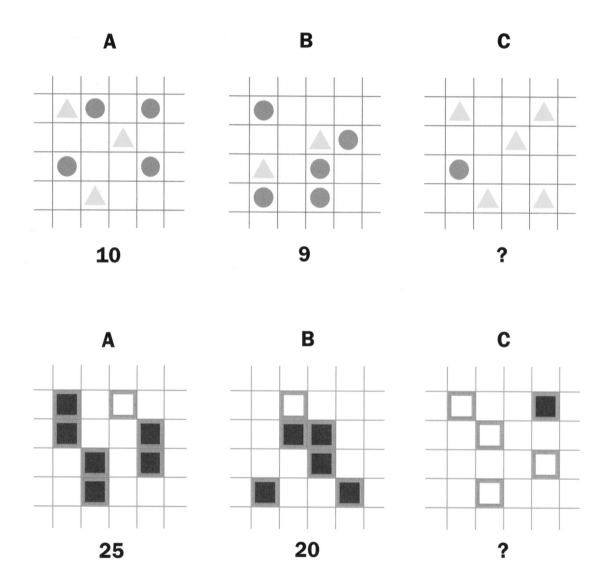

180

PUZZLE 255

Which of the following is the odd one out?

Answers see page **219**

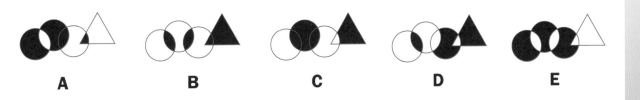

A   **B**   **C**   **D**   **E**

PUZZLE 256

Which of the following is the odd one out?

Answers see page **219**

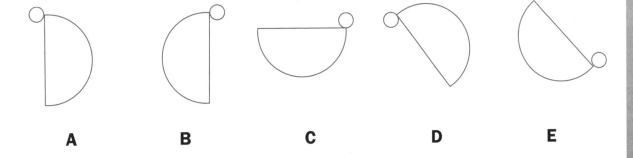

A   **B**   **C**   **D**   **E**

PUZZLE 257

Which of the following is the odd one out?

Answers see page **219**

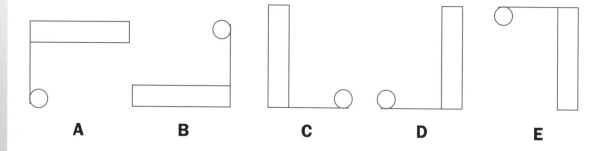

A **B** **C** **D** **E**

PUZZLE 258

Which of the following is the odd one out?

Answers see page **219**

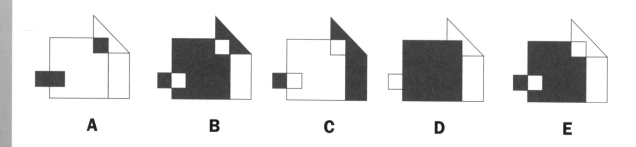

A **B** **C** **D** **E**

PUZZLE 259

Which of the following is the odd one out?

Answers see page **219**

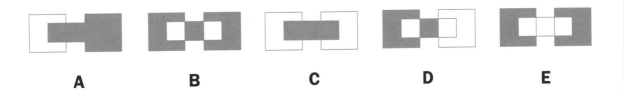

A   **B**   **C**   **D**   **E**

PUZZLE 260

Which of the following is the odd one out?

Answers see page **219**

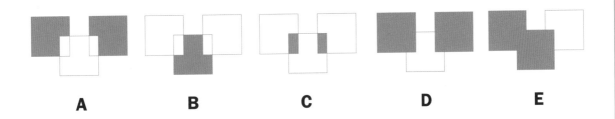

A   **B**   **C**   **D**   **E**

PUZZLE 261

Which of the following is the odd one out?

Answers see page **219**

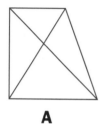 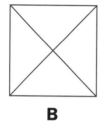  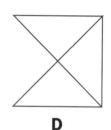 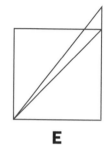

A　　　**B**　　　**C**　　　**D**　　　**E**

PUZZLE 262

Which of the following is the odd one out?

Answers see page **219**

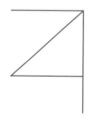 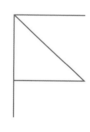 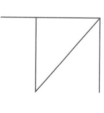 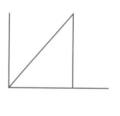 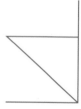

A　　　**B**　　　**C**　　　**D**　　　**E**

PUZZLE 263

Which of the following is the odd one out?

Answers see page **219**

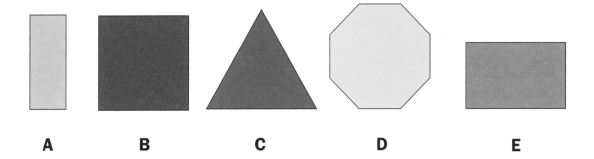

PUZZLE 264

Which of the following is the odd one out?

Answers see page **219**

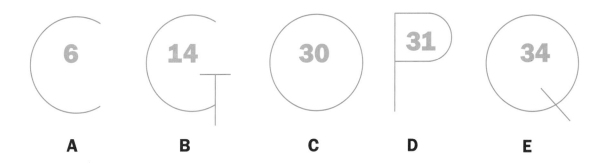

PUZZLE 265

Should A, B, C, or D fill the empty circle?

Answers see page **219**

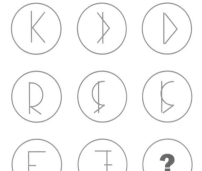

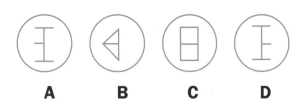

A   **B**   **C**   **D**

PUZZLE 266

Should A, B, C, or D fill the empty circle?

Answers see page **219**

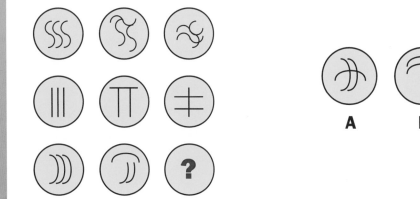

A   **B**   **C**   **D**

PUZZLE 267

Should A, B, C, or D fill the empty circle?

Answers see page **219**

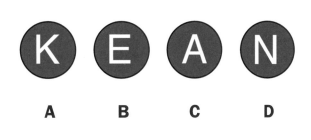

PUZZLE 268

Should A, B, C, or D fill the empty circle?

Answers see page **219**

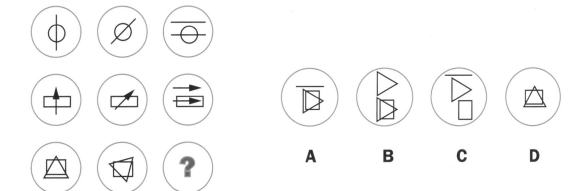

PUZZLE 269

Should A, B, C, or D fill the empty circle?

Answers see page **219**

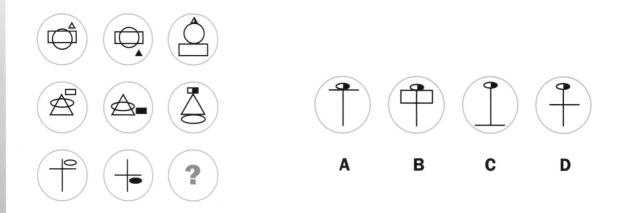

PUZZLE 270

No symbol is used on more than one side of the box. Which of these is not a view of the same box?

Answers see page **219**

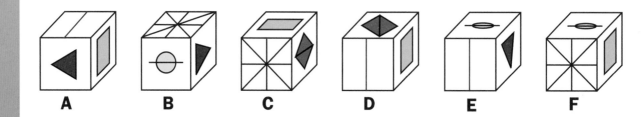

PUZZLE 271

No symbol is used on more than one side of the box. Which of these is not a view of the same box?

Answers see page **219**

  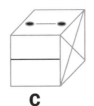   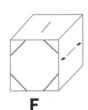

A **B** **C** **D** **E** **F**

PUZZLE 272

No symbol is used on more than one side of the box. Which of these is not a view of the same box?

Answers see page **219**

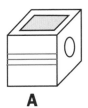  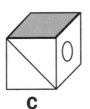  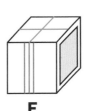 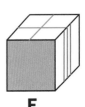

A **B** **C** **D** **E** **F**

PUZZLE 273

No symbol is used on more than one side of the box. Which of these is not a view of the same box?

Answers see page **219**

 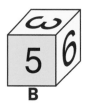    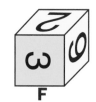

A   B   C   D   E   F

PUZZLE 274

No symbol is used on more than one side of the box. Which of these is not a view of the same box?

Answers see page **219**

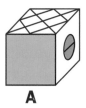 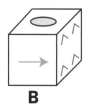 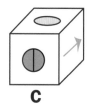 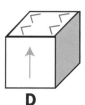 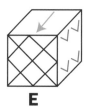 

A   B   C   D   E   F

PUZZLE 275

Which of these boxes can be made from the template? Is it A, B, C, D, E, or F?

Answers see page **219**

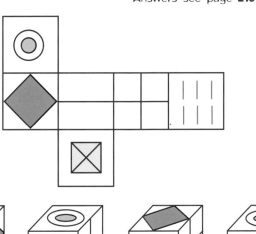

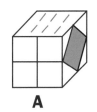 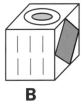   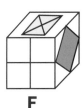

A   **B**   **C**   **D**   **E**   **F**

PUZZLE 276

Which of these boxes can be made from the template? Is it A, B, C, D, E, or F?

Answers see page **219**

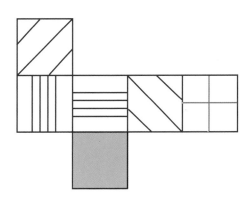

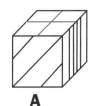 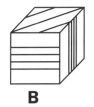 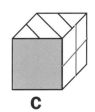  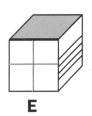 

A   **B**   **C**   **D**   **E**   **F**

PUZZLE 277

Which of these boxes can be made from the template? Is it A, B, C, D, E, or F?

Answers see page **219**

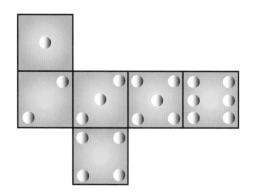

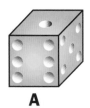
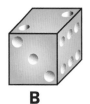
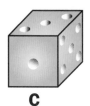
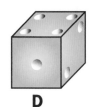
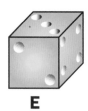
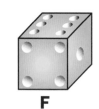

A **B** **C** **D** **E** **F**

PUZZLE 278

Which of these boxes can be made from the template? Is it A, B, C, D, E, or F?

Answers see page **219**

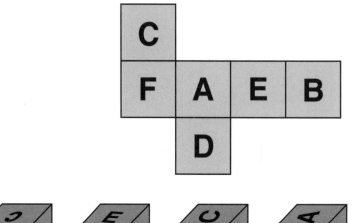

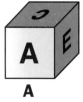
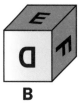
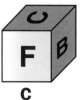
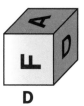
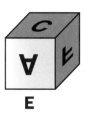
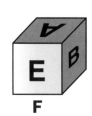

A **B** **C** **D** **E** **F**

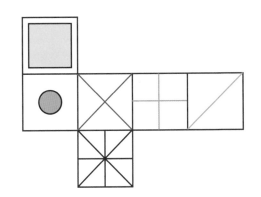

PUZZLE 279

Which of these boxes can be made from the template? Is it A, B, C, D, E, or F?

Answers see page **219**

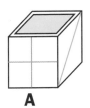 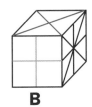  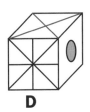 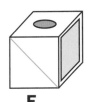 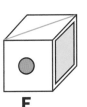

A   **B**   **C**   **D**   **E**   **F**

PUZZLE 280 Example

These are all mirror image problems. One of the four given images has an error on it.

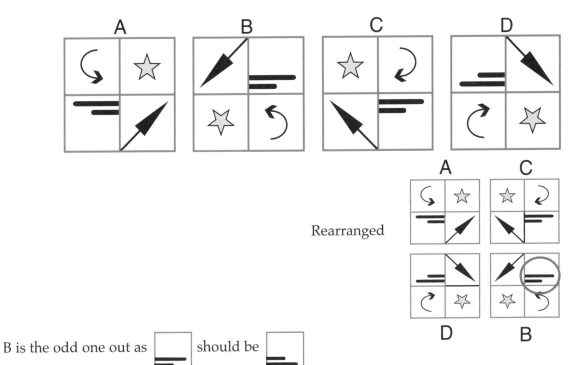

Rearranged

B is the odd one out as [   ] should be [   ]

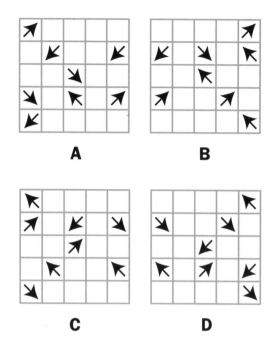

PUZZLE 280

These are all mirror image problems. One of the four given images has an error on it.

Answers see page **219**

PUZZLE 281

These are all mirror image problems. One of the four given images has an error on it.

Answers see page **219**

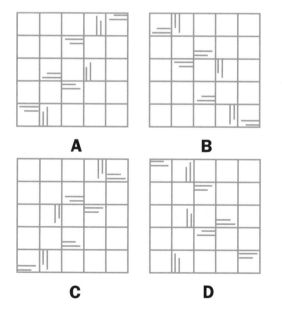

A **B**

PUZZLE 282

These are all mirror image problems. One of the four given images has an error on it.

Answers see page **219**

C **D**

PUZZLE 283

These are all mirror image problems. One of the four given images has an error on it.

Answers see page **219**

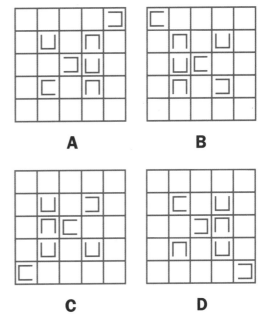

A **B**

C **D**

195

PUZZLE 284

These are all mirror image problems. One of the four given images has an error on it.

Answers see page **219**

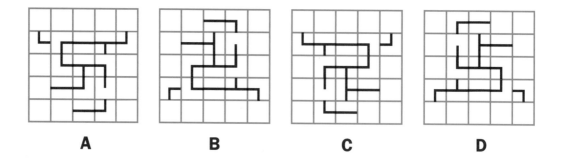

A **B** **C** **D**

PUZZLE 285

Answers see page **220**

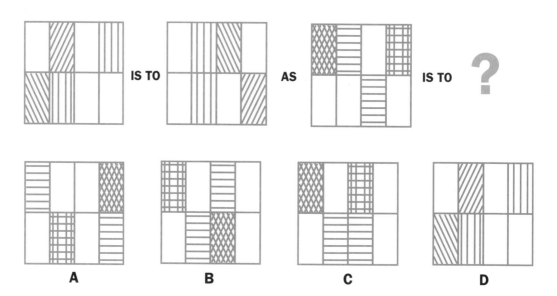

A **B** **C** **D**

PUZZLE 286

Answers see page 220

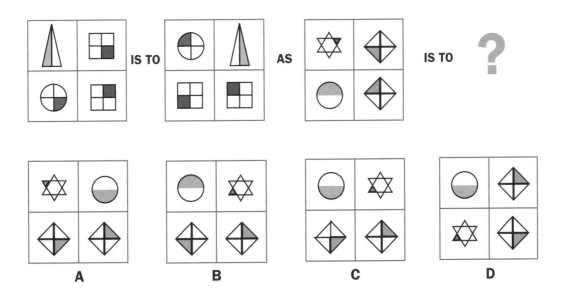

A   B   C   D

PUZZLE 287

Answers see page 220

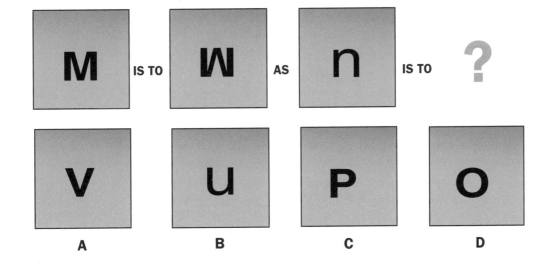

A   B   C   D

PUZZLE 288

Answers see page **220**

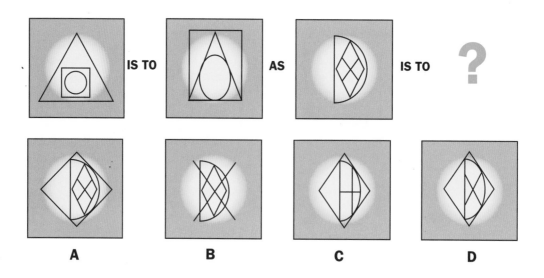

PUZZLE 289

Answers see page **220**

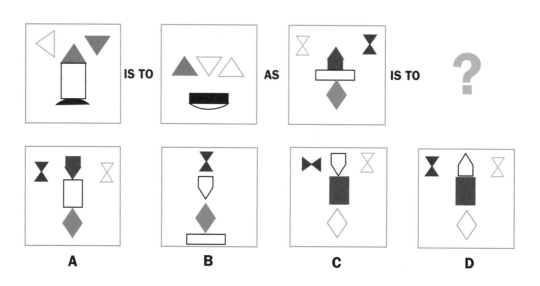

PUZZLE 290

Which of the shapes A, B, C, D, or E cannot be made from the dots if a line is drawn through all of the dots at least once?

Answers see page **220**

A   **B**   **C**   **D**   **E**

PUZZLE 291

Which of the shapes A, B, C, D, or E cannot be made from the dots if a line is drawn through all of the dots at least once?

Answers see page **220**

A   **B**   **C**   **D**   **E**

PUZZLE 292

Which of the shapes A, B, C, D, or E cannot be made from the dots if a line is drawn through all of the dots at least once?

Answers see page **220**

A　　**B**　　**C**　　**D**　　**E**

PUZZLE 293

Which of the shapes A, B, C, D, or E cannot be made from the dots if a line is drawn through all of the dots at least once?

Answers see page **220**

  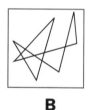  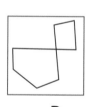 

A　　**B**　　**C**　　**D**　　**E**

PUZZLE 294

Which of the shapes A, B, C, D, or E cannot be made from the dots if a line is drawn through all of the dots at least once?

Answers see page **220**

A   **B**   **C**   **D**   **E**

PUZZLE 295

Should A, B, C, or D come next in this series?

Answers see page **220**

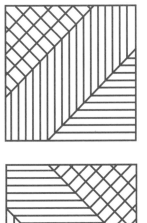 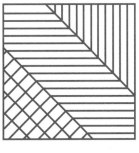 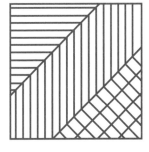 

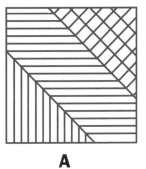 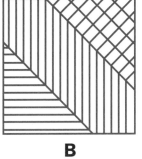 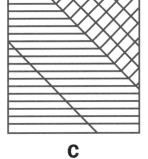 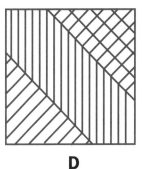

A   **B**   **C**   **D**

PUZZLE 296

Answers see page **220**

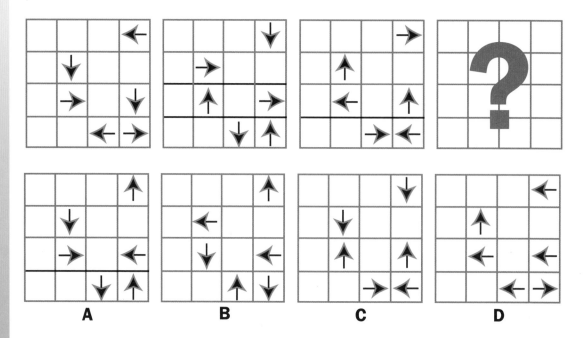

PUZZLE 297

Answers see page **220**

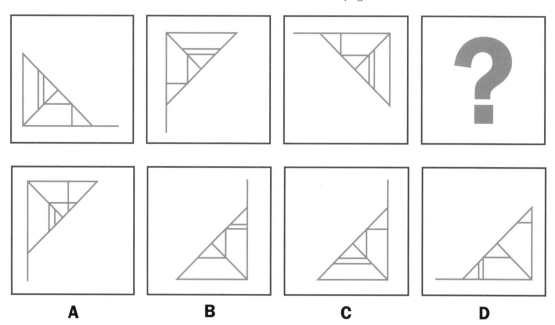

PUZZLE 298

Answers see page **220**

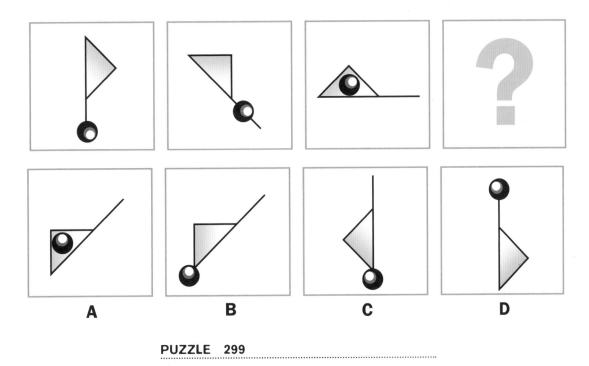

A   B   C   D

PUZZLE 299

Answers see page **220**

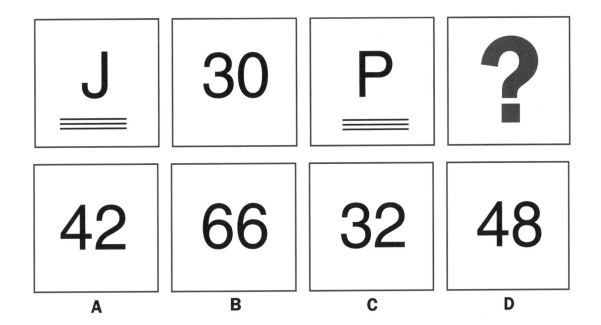

A   B   C   D

PUZZLE 300

Answers see page **220**

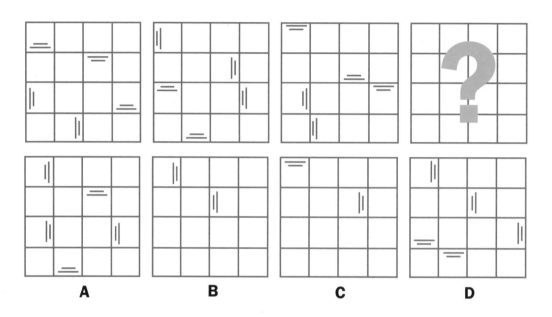

A   B   C   D

PUZZLE 301

Answers see page **220**

HB28	DC34	GA17	?
EI95	EI90	EI85	EI100
A	B	C	D

PUZZLE 302

Answers see page **220**

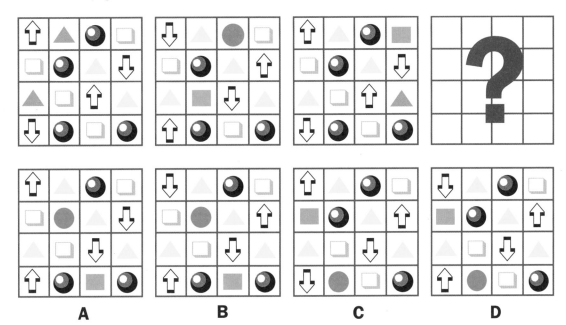

A   B   C   D

PUZZLE 303

Answers see page **220**

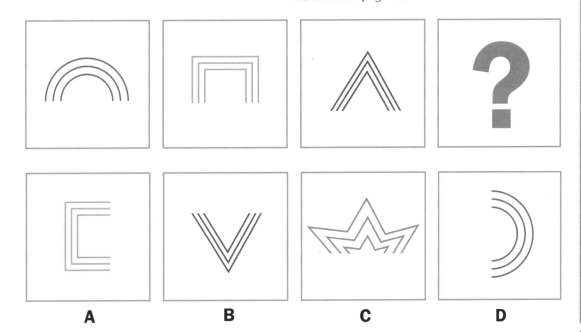

A   B   C   D

PUZZLE 304

Draw a pentagon, and connect each point with every other point by straight lines, as in the diagram. How many different triangles are contained in this figure?

Answers see page **220**

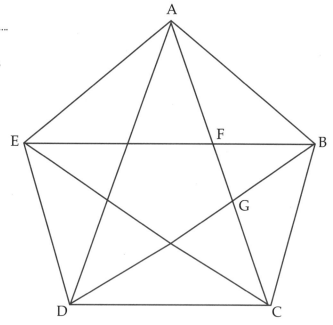

PUZZLE 305

A life prisoner appealed to the king for pardon. Not being ready to grant the appeal the king proposed a pardon on condition that the prisoner should start from cell A and go in and out of each cell in the prison, coming back to cell A without going in any cell twice. How could it be done?

Answers see page **220**

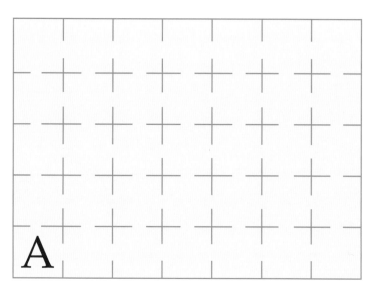

PUZZLE 306

Here is a piece of land marked off with 36 circular plots, on each of which is deposited a bag containing as many gold coins as the figures indicated in the diagram. You are allowed to pick up as many bags as you like, provided that you do not take two lying on the same line. What is the largest amount of money you can pick up?

Answers see page **220**

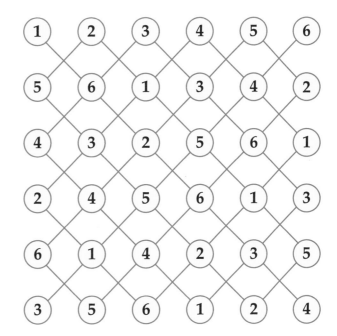

PUZZLE 307

The diagram represents a simplified railway system and you have to find how many different ways there are of getting from A to E if you never go along the same line in any journey.

Answers see page **220**

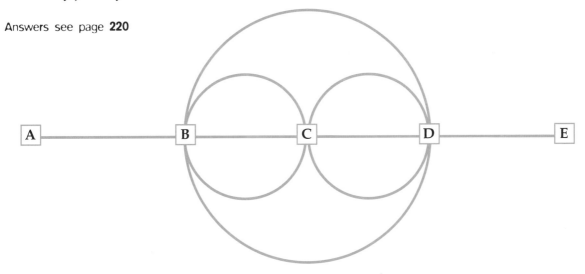

PUZZLE 308

A man started to drive from town A and wished to make a complete tour of roads, going along every one of them once only. How many different routes are there from which he can select? Every route must end at town A, from which you start, and you must go straight from town to town never turning off at crossroads.

Answers see page **220**

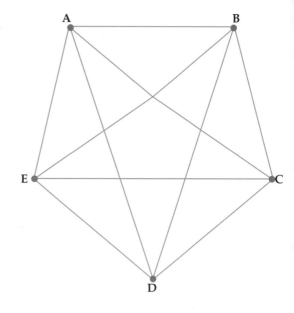

PUZZLE 309

A merchant had ten barrels of sugar that he placed in a pyramid, as shown. Every barrel bore a different number, except one, which was not marked. You can see that he had accidentally arranged them so that the numbers in the three sides all added up to 16. Can you rearrange them so that the sides shall add up to the smallest number possible? The central barrel does not count.

Answers see page **221**

PUZZLE 310

The sixteen squares of a miniature chessboard are enclosed by 16 matches. You have to place an *odd* number of matches inside the square so as to enclose four groups of four squares each. There are four ways of doing this.

Answers see page **221**

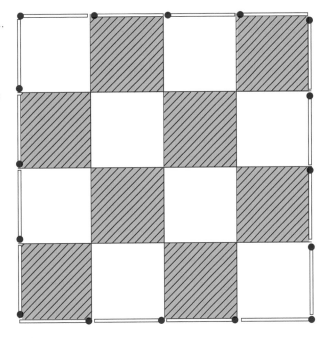

PUZZLE 311

In the diagram the numbers 1 to 19 are arranged so that all twelve lines of three add up to 23. Six of these lines are, of course, the six sides, and the other six lines radiate from the centre. Can you find an arrangement that will still add up to 23 in all twelve directions? There is only one way to do it.

Answers see page **221**

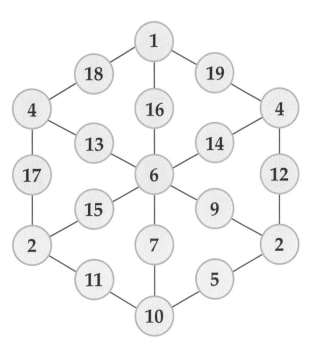

PUZZLE 312

Draw this design of a circle and triangles in as few continuous strokes as possible. You may go over a line twice if you wish, and begin and end wherever you like.

Answers see page **221**

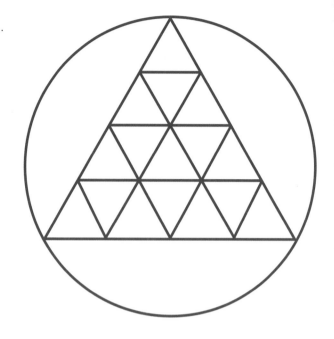

PUZZLE 313

In this square, as every cell contains the same number - 1234 - the three columns, three rows, and two long diagonals naturally add up alike. The puzzle is to form and place nine different four-figure numbers (using the same figures) so that they shall form a perfect magic square. Remember that the numbers must contain nine of each figure 1, 2, 3, 4 and you cannot use fractions or any form of trickery.

Answers see page **221**

1234	1234	1234
1234	1234	1234
1234	1234	1234

PUZZLE 314

This is a field in which grow 16 trees. The eccentric farmer decided to erect five straight fences so that every tree should have a separate enclosure. How did he do it?

Answers see page **221**

PUZZLE 315

Place the numbers 1 to 19 in the 19 circles so that wherever there are three in a straight line they shall add up to 30.

Answers see page **221**

Mind Marathon

Answers

Answer 184

1. Player 2.
2. Player 3.
3. Player 6.
4. Player 3.
5. Players 1 and 5.
6. Players 1, 4 and 6.
7. 21.
8. 46.

Answer 185

 □ = 3 ▲ = 5 ◯ = 2 ⌀ = 7 ● = 4 ★ = 1 ■ = 6

Answer 186

2. (A x B) – (D x E) = C
(B x C) + A = (D x E)

Answer 187

A. 97. Position of hands (not time) with hour hand, first, expressed as a sum.
113 – 16 = 97.
Others are: 51 + 123 = 174, 911 + 82 = 993.

B. 36. Position of hands (not time), expressed as minute hand – hour hand, then do sum.
(2 – 11) [–9] x (8 – 12) [–4] = 36.
Others are: (12 – 3)[9] x (7 – 5) [2] = 18, (6 – 2) [4] x (8 – 1) [7] = 28.

C. 16. Sum of segment values of shaded parts.

D. 216. Position of hands (not time), added together, then do sum.
(3 + 9) [12] x (12 + 6) [18] = 216.
Others are: (12 + 6) [18] + (6 + 3) [9] = 27,
(12 + 9) [21] – (9 + 6)[15] = 6.

Answer 188

A. 2. Make sums: First 2 digits – Second 2 digits, then First – Second.

B. 280. First digit x Fourth digit = First and Fourth digits, Second digit x Third digit = Second and Third digits.

C. 28. First digit x Second digit = First and Second digits, and Third digit x Fourth digit = Third and Fourth Digits.

Answer 189

A.

8	7	6	8	7	12	9	1
7	12	7	6	4	3	2	14
8	9	7	8	5	7	11	1
8	8	10	7	6	16	10	1
4	9	13	4	12	2	15	6
8	5	2	2	4	9	8	15
6	9	8	14	14	8	2	1
9	6	10	5	12	1	5	17

B.

5	7	8	15	4	7	5	6
11	6	9	8	16	12	10	10
7	12	10	12	3	11	6	8
6	7	2	5	7	7	15	10
12	15	10	8	5	12	8	7
6	7	11	13	9	6	9	6
9	8	10	6	8	8	1	2
3	6	4	10	10	10	15	15

Answer 190

1. 40.

	4	5	12	13	
	3	6	11	14	
	2	7	10	15	
	1	8	9	16	

2. 36.

16	9	8	1
15	10	7	2
14	11	6	3
13	12	5	4

3. 41. The grid values are the same as for answer 2.

Answer 191
68. (Top left^2 – Bottom right) + (Bottom left^2 – Top right).
126. (Top left + Top right + Bottom left) – Bottom right.

Answer 192
1. 17—19—22—24—28—20 = 130
2. 17—19—22—28—25—20 = 131
   17—23—22—24—25—20 = 131
3. 140. 17—24—26—28—25—20
4. 127. 17—19—22—24—25—20

Answer 193
1. 35—34—34—34—35—34—10
2. 35—32—29—28—37—33—10
   35—30—29—35—32—33—10
3. 219. 35—34—34—35—37—34—10
4. 202. 35—30—29—28—37—33—10
5. 4 ways: 35—32—29—35—37—33—10
   35—30—34—35—32—35—10
   35—33—32—34—32—35—10
   35—33—32—32—35—34—10

Answer 194
A. 29. Green = 7; White = 3; Shaded = 9.
B. 25. Green = 4; White = 5; Shaded = 6.
C. 25. Green = 5; White = 2; Shaded = 8.

Answer 195
A. 26.
B. 36.
C. 34.
D. D4 = 70.
E. 16.
F. 4. (A6, B6).

G. = 8   ● = 20

H. A2, C1, D6.

	A	B	C	D	E	F
1	28	28	32	26	16	8
2	32	●	52	46	⊤	16
3	36	44	□	64	42	34
4	26	⊤	56	70	□	40
5	16	16	34	48	●	36
6	4	4	22	32	28	28

Answer 196
A. △ = 16   ⊙ = 24   ★ = 10

B. 102. D3.
C. 89.
D. 20. F6
E. 73.
F. Two, C5 and D5.

	A	B	C	D	E	F
1	△	46	54	54	49	24
2	33	58	★	△	△	36
3	37	62	⊙	102	73	48
4	41	69	89	89	⊙	48
5	36	⊙	64	64	52	32
6	24	32	52	△	28	20

Answer 197
(In answers A–D, n = previous number)
A. 35. (n + 3), (n + 6), (n + 9), etc.
B. 1125. Multiply the previous two numbers.
C. 94. (2n + 3), (2n + 6), (2n + 9), etc.
D. 666. (n^2 – 10).

Answer 198
A. 120. Sum of left x sum of right.
B. –18. (Left numbers multiplied) – (right numbers multiplied).
C. 10. ((Outside top x outside bottom) – Inside). Left side – right side.

Answer 199
A.   A6, C5, G6.
B.   D2.
C.   12.
D.   117, occurs 3 times.
E.   91, G1.
F.   E4.
G.   None.
H.   None.

Answer 200
A. 175. (Window + Window) x Door.
B. 42. (Left window x Right window) – Door.
C. 71. (Left window x Door) + Right window.
D. 60. (Right window – Door) x Left window.

Answer 201
C. Others rotate into the same shape.

Answer 202
D. A & E and B & C form opposite pairs.

Answer 203
C. Others are Roman numerals rotated 90° clockwise.

Answer 204
D. Others rotate into the same shape.

Answer 205
E. Others rotate into the same shape.

Answer 206
A. Others rotate into the same shape.

Answer 207
B. A & D and C & E form opposite pairs.

Answer 208
E. It contains four lines; the others have only three.

Answer 209
D. The pattern inside does not go clockwise.

Answer 210
E. It is the only one with an enclosed space.

Answer 211
A. Binary system, start at 5 and add 3 each time. You can also find the answer by treating the images as a negative and mirror-imaging them.

Answer 212
B. Numbers rotate clockwise by the number given.

Answer 213
E. The figures rotate one sector at a time.

Answer 214
B. Shapes rotate in sequence. The square changes colour.

Answer 215
A. Shapes rotate in sequence.

Answer 216
B. All use three lines.

Answer 217
C. Rotates and lines are subtracted from one and added to the other.

Answer 218
D. Rotating circle and lines.

Answer 219
D. Small circles move left to right and bottom to top.

Answer 220
A. Each shape rotates in a set sequence.

Answer 221
D. Matched opposite pairs.

Answer 222
D. Whole figure rotates 90° anti- (counter) clockwise and circles are reversed at end of lines.

Answer 223
C. Rotations in sequence.

Answer 224
D. First number is alpha-numeric position (eg, A=1).

Answer 225
A. D.
B. B.
C. C.
D. A.

Answer 226
A.   D.
B.   B.
C.   B.
D.   E.
E.   C.

Answer 227
C.

Answer 228
F.

Answer 229
E.

Answer 230
A.

Answer 231
F.

Answer 232
E.

Answer 233
G.

Answer 234
F.

Answer 235
E. Duplicated lines on first two of each row are deleted in third figure.

Answer 236
E. • = (numbers of stars x 2) + numbers of stars = number of stars in column 3.

Answer 237
E.

Answer 238
A.

Answer 239
D.

Answer 240
E.

Answer 241
B.

Answer 242
A. 3.87. 116 passes for 30 students.
B. 3.32. 83 passes for 25 students.
C. 58.

Answer 243
42. = 17   = 5   ■ = 15

Answer 244
328. Along each row multiply first two digits of first number to get first two digits of second number. Multiply last two digits of first number to get last two of second number and join them. 4 x 8 = 32, 2 x 4 = 8; 328.

Answer 245
4752. In each number the first two digits are multiplied by the last two digits to give the next number along the row. 54 x 88 = 4752.

Answer 246
184. In each row the two outer digits of the first number are multiplied to give the two outer digits of the second number. The two middle of the first number are multiplied to give the middle digits of the second number. 7 x 2 =14; 4 x 2 = 8; 184.

Answer 247
A. 3. (A + B) x C = D + E.
B. 3. (A + C) – (D x E) = B or A – B + C ÷ D = E.
C. 0 and 6. B + D = E ; E – A = C.

Answer 248
A. 3 white circles. Purple circle values are:
Top = 1, right = 2, bottom = 3, left = 4.
Values are then added. White circle = 5.
Sums are (1 + 3) x (4 + 1) = 20. (4 + 1) x (1 + 2) = 15. (4 + 1) + (2 + 3) = 10. (3 + 4 + 1) – (1 + 2) = 5.

B. 6 circles. ★ = 3, n = 1.5, ◯ = 2.

217

Answer 249

A. 1625. Add times as numbers. 135 + 600 = 735; 245 + 1215 = 1460;
520 + 1105 = 1625.

B. 294. Add numbers on pointers and complete the sum. (6 + 9) [15] x (1 + 6) [7] = 105; (6 + 3) [9] x (9 + 3) [12] = 108; (12 + 9) [21] x (2 + 12) [14] = 294.

Answer 250

A. 1560. Add times as numbers. 200 + 730 = 930; 245 + 445 = 690;
915 + 645 = 1560.

B. 32. Multiply the hands by their sector values and complete the sum.

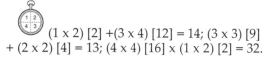 (1 x 2) [2] +(3 x 4) [12] = 14; (3 x 3) [9] + (2 x 2) [4] = 13; (4 x 4) [16] x (1 x 2) [2] = 32.

Answer 251

Top.

18	6	4	30	47	29
45	30	6	18	17	2
1	21	1	42	23	5
3	28	7	17	1	6
44	4	32	43	30	40

Bottom.

6	2	3	4	4	3
3	5	5	2	6	2
5	3	1	3	5	0
2	4	5	3	0	5
3	3	4	6	6	5

Answer 252

Top. 4.The two-digit number on the left minus the two-digit number on the right gives the middle number.

Bottom. 4.The two-digit number on the right minus the two-digit number on the left gives the middle number.

Answer 253

Top.
Add the two digits of each number together to give the number of places the numbers move round.

	34	
21		14
	55	

Bottom.
Add one to each number to give the amount of places each number moves around.

3		4
5		2

Answer 254

Top.
Eleven. The values are totalled in each grid to give the number shown. The sum of the values of triangles and circles gives the answer. Δ = 2, O = 1.

Bottom.
–15. The sum of the values of white and purple squares gives the answer.

Answer 255
C. Others are matched opposite pairs.

Answer 256
B. Others rotate into each other.

Answer 257
D. Others rotate into each other.

Answer 258
E. Has only two segments shaded; the others have three.

Answer 259
E. Only one with middle square white.

Answer 260
E. Not symmetrical around a vertical middle.

Answer 261
D. Others have six lines.

Answer 262
A. Others rotate into each other.

Answer 263
C. Not symmetrical around horizontal axis.

Answer 264
D. Number denotes twice the alphabetical position.

Answer 265
D. Letter reverses, vertical line moves to the left.

Answer 266
C. One vertical line moves to a horizontal position, then two lines move to a horizontal position.

Answer 267
B. First letter contains two straight lines, second letter contains three straight lines, and third letter contains four straight lines.

Answer 268
B. Vertical object moves 45° clockwise, then a further 45° clockwise, then doubles.

Answer 269
C. Horizontal object moves down, small shape moves down then up again.

Answer 270
A.

Answer 271
B.

Answer 272
D.

Answer 273
D.

Answer 274
E.

Answer 275
B.

Answer 276
C.

Answer 277
E.

Answer 278
D

Answer 279
A.

Answer 280
B.

Answer 281
D.

Answer 282
D.

Answer 283
C.

Answer 284
A.

Answer 285
A. Move sections three places clockwise.

Answer 286
C. Boxes rotate clockwise and opposite segments are shaded.

Answer 287
B. Same upside-down.

Answer 288
D. Inside shapes get longer and outside shape moves inside middle shape.

Answer 289
C. White shapes turn 90° clockwise. Coloured shapes turn 180°. Coloured becomes white and white becomes black.

Answer 290
B & E.

Answer 291
C.

Answer 292
D.

Answer 293
E.

Answer 294
A.

Answer 295
A. Box rotates 90° anti- (counter) clockwise.

Answer 296
B. Each segment rotates 90° anti- (counter) clockwise.

Answer 297
C. Turns 90° clockwise.

Answer 298
B. Turns 45° anti- (counter) clockwise, circle moves along.

Answer 299
D. Alpha position multiplied by the number of lines.

Answer 300
D. Short and long lines swap places and rotate clockwise.

Answer 301
A. Alpha values reversed.

Answer 302
D. Arrows reverse direction. Shading moves one place.

Answer 303
C. Lines point down.

Answer 304
35.

Answer 305
Follow the diagram as shown until you reach point B. Then place one foot in C and say, 'As one foot has been in cell C it has undoubtedly been entered. However, when that foot is withdrawn into B I do not enter B for a second time because I never left it.'

Answer 306
47 coins contained in 10 bags all deposited on outside plots, thus 4, 5 and 6 in the first row, 5 in the second, 4 in the third, 3 in the fourth, 5 in the fifth, and 5, 6, 4 in the bottom row.

Answer 307
There are 2501 possible routes.

Answer 308
There are 264 routes.

Answer 309

Arrange the barrels in one of the following two ways and the sides will add up to 13 in either case.

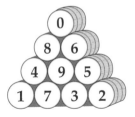 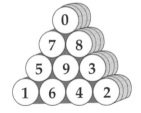

Answer 310

The diagram shows how to complete the task using 11 matches.

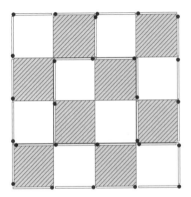

Answer 311

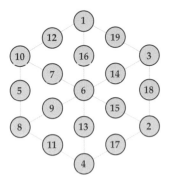

Answer 312

You can do this with 14 strokes, starting from A and ending at Z.

Answer 313

2243	1341	3142
3141	2242	1343
1342	3143	2241

Answer 314

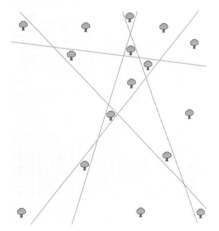

Answer 315

All you have to do is place 10 in the centre and write in their proper order round the circle 1, 2, 3, 4, 5, 6, 7, 8, 9, 19, 18, 17, 16, 15, 14, 13, 12, 11.

Colour Conundrums

In this section you will find some innovations. For the first time in this series we have used crosswords (all with a colour theme), and mazes. There are also numerous puzzles where your task will be to work out just what the significance of the colours might be, and that won't be nearly as easy as you might think. This section will be challenging, different and fun. Enjoy!

PUZZLE 316

Would you put the pink smiley in column 1 or column 2?

Answers see page **252**

1   2

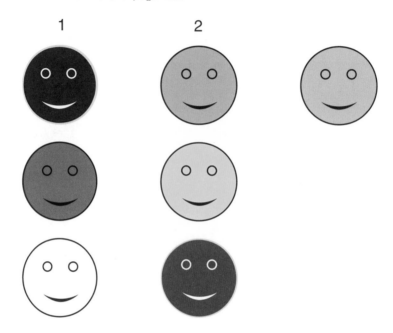

A	S	C	O	T
O	D	G	L	M
H	O	U	E	A
E	K	R	N	L
S	M	C	G	A
T	E	A	N	V
I	D	J	O	Y

PUZZLE 317

The grid below contains the name of a European country. To find it you must move from square to touching square (including diagonals). To help you, colours making up the name have something in common.

Answers see page **252**

T	J	S	H	I	V
K	S	D	J	M	E
S	S	R	T	A	Z
G	E	L	I	S	A
H	M	I	Q	D	D
M	E	X	T	W	L
N	V	L	C	G	K

PUZZLE 318

The following is a coded message. The only clue you get is that the answer is related to the colours used.

Answers see page **252**

PUZZLE 319

These objects can be arranged in a logical order in which the black square is first and the yellow hexagon is last. What is the order?

Answers see page **252**

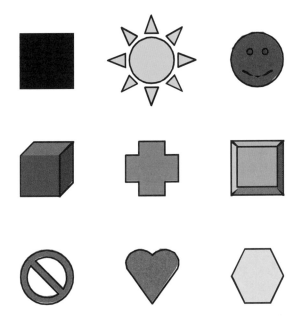

PUZZLE 320

There is a logic to the placing of the
coloured hearts and the accompanying
numbers. If you can work it out you will
be able to replace the question mark with a
number.

Answers see page **252**

19

7

12

?

PUZZLE 321

These coloured blocks can be rearranged to
create a logical order. Red is still the first in
the series and yellow the last. What is the
order of the other colours?

Answers see page **252**

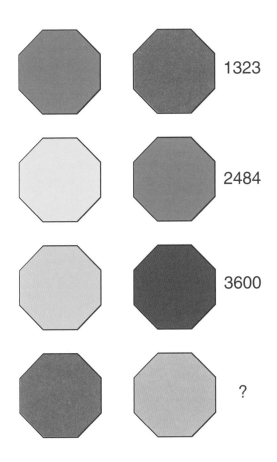

1323

2484

3600

?

PUZZLE 322

To find the missing number you need to discover the significance of the coloured shapes.

Answers see page **252**

PUZZLE 323

Which of these shapes is the odd one out?

Answers see page **252**

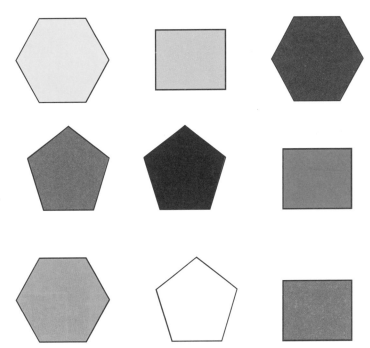

PUZZLE 324

There is a logic to the shapes, colours and numbers below. See if you can discover how it works and then find the missing number.

Answers see page **252**

276

54

368

81

184

196

147

98

?

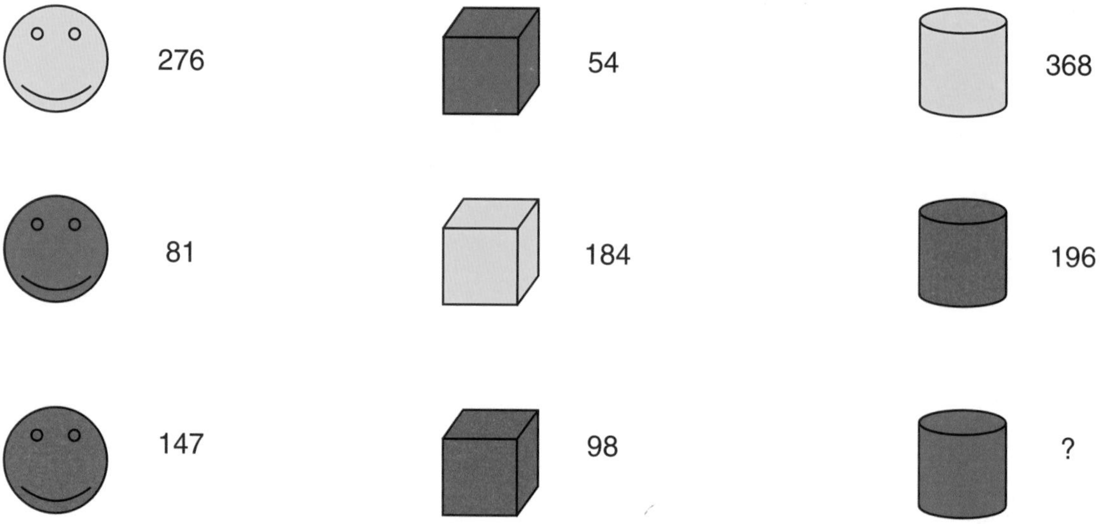

PUZZLE 325

There is a logic to the shapes, colours and numbers below. See if you can discover how it works and then find the missing number.

Answers see page **252**

50

83

45

78

35

25

30

55

?

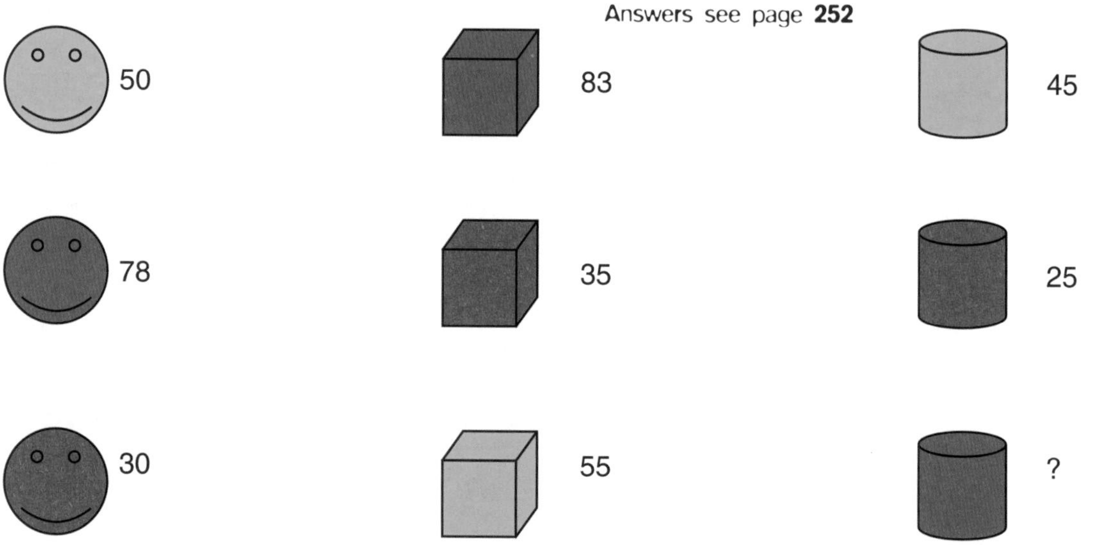

T I O D U

I T N O E E

W C H O F T

E R S N T R

O N W N S I

PUZZLE 326

The letters can be rearranged to make a well-known Shakespearean phrase. The colours will help you.

Answers see page **252**

PUZZLE 327

The numbers under the coloured rings have a significance, but what is it? When you have worked it out you will be able to replace the question mark with a number.

Answers see page **252**

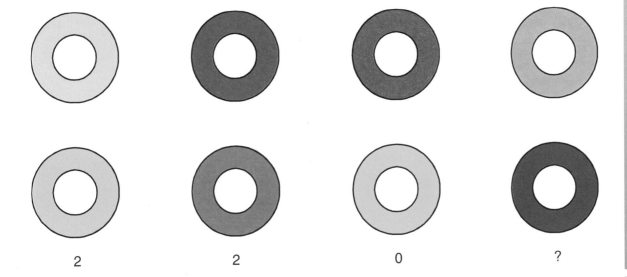

2   2   0   ?

PUZZLE 328

The numbers are in some way related to the coloured squares. If you can work out the relationship you will be able to replace the question mark with a number.

Answers see page **252**

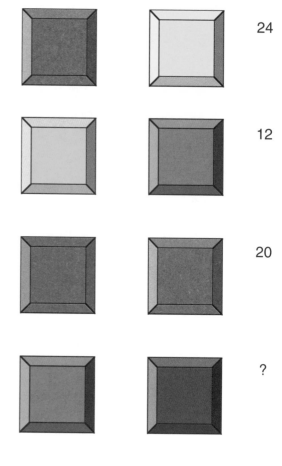

R G E H D

Q I T S T

V H P E S

C T O L M

O X U T R

PUZZLE 329

This is a really simple code that depends on the colours of the letters for its solution.

Answers see page **252**

PUZZLE 330

The letters conceal a well-known phrase
from a Shakespeare play. The letters of
each word are the same colour, though
they have been mixed up. Letters of other
colours have been introduced to add
confusion.

Answers see page **252**

W	T	T	D	J
A	S	H	M	H
U	O	G	A	I
E	T	L	E	R
T	E	W	O	D
O	F	H	U	T
O	R	H	S	P
R	O	A	Y	O
E	D	I	A	M
R	P	E	J	H

PUZZLE 331

If the following says
THREE WHEELER FOLLOWS VEGAN,

What do the characters below say?
The letters have been mixed up but all
letters of the same colour belong together.

Answers see page **252**

PUZZLE 332

The colours all have a numerical value, though this time it is rather an unusual one. Just one of the shapes also has a numerical significance. When you have worked out what the colours and shapes mean you will be able to find the missing number.

Answers see page **252**

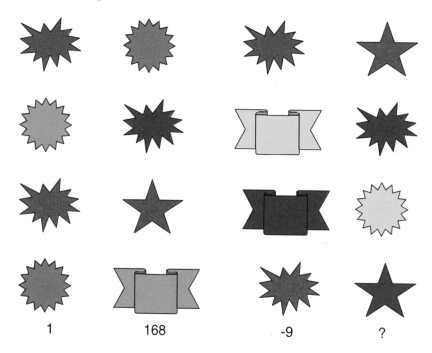

1   168   -9   ?

PUZZLE 333

The grid contains a famous name (but not that famous, so you'll need help to find it). You need to move from square to touching square (including diagonals). The colours of the letters used in the name have something in common.

Answers see page **252**

S	H	K	E	N	A	W	O	L	Y
O	Y	A	K	R	S	A	L	W	T
R	A	W	L	O	W	I	B	P	F
T	L	I	B	J	O	L	N	A	S
U	P	C	T	T	N	E	A	S	O
L	U	A	N	L	G	M	R	B	T
A	D	B	E	A	M	O	C	E	A
N	R	P	I	T	L	T	I	P	D
O	E	J	H	B	S	F	N	U	U
G	L	I	S	P	E	T	A	M	J

PUZZLE 334

The direction in which the arrows point is in some way related to their colour. Would an orange arrow point up or down?

Answers see page **252**

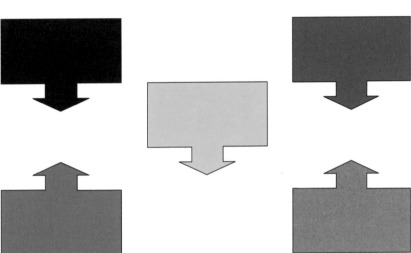

7	12	19	2	18	14	5
8	9	18	26	4	18	21
15	17	12	15	9	25	22
19	7	26	24	19	8	14
9	23	13	19	6	7	12
23	5	22	3	21	15	24
12	23	10	14	11	15	22

PUZZLE 335

The numbers contain a hidden message. What is it?

Answers see page **252**

158

PUZZLE 336

These colours and shapes all have a numerical significance. Once you work out what it is you will be able to find the missing number.

     148

Answers see page **252-3**

    20?

    ?

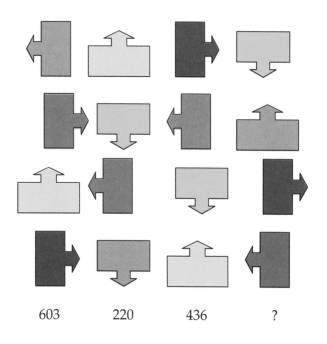

603   220   436   ?

PUZZLE 337

Each of the colours has a numerical value. The shapes affect this value in some way. Discover the connection between shape and colour and you will be able to find the missing number.

Answers see page **253**

234

PUZZLE 338

There is a message hidden in the table below. If you can work out which colours to use you will be able to read it.

Answers see page **253**

A	M	P	N	O	S
T	Z	J	H	K	B
E	R	C	U	V	O
N	J	T	N	V	L
I	N	Q	G	C	R
D	O	G	L	D	X
E	P	F	X	S	Q

T	X	B	Q	H
M	K	I	S	D
R	O	N	E	S
I	S	G	A	B
I	X	B	T	E
F	H	G	A	L
R	D	P	D	L
J	P	E	R	S

PUZZLE 339

This is a simple coded message that depends on colours for its solution.

Answers see page **253**

PUZZLE 340

Find the shortest path from START to END.

Answers see page **253**

PUZZLE 341

Find the shortest path from START to END.

Answers see page **253**

PUZZLE 342

Find the shortest path from START to END.

Answers see page **253**

PUZZLE 343

Find the shortest path from START to END.

Answers see page **253**

PUZZLE 344

Find the shortest path from START to END.

Answers see page **254**

PUZZLE   345

Find the shortest path from START to END.

Answers see page **254**

PUZZLE 346

The two pictures are identical except for ten alterations made to the second version. See if you can spot the ten differences.

Answers see page **254**

PUZZLE 347

The two pictures are identical except for ten alterations made to the second version. See if you can spot the ten differences.

Answers see page **254**

PUZZLE 348

The two pictures are identical except for ten alterations made to the second version. See if you can spot the ten differences.

Answers see page **255**

PUZZLE 349

Answers see page **255**

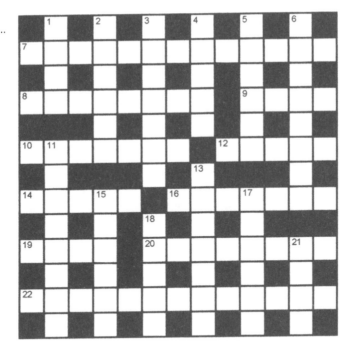

ACROSS

7   Which Hugh? Sounds like there are so many! (5-8)

8   In arid conditions fern may become invisible (8)

9   Got a deconstructed dress? (4)

10 French Ebenezer loses young Benjamin to make you blue (7)

12 Colourful genre? (5)

14 Gaberdine needs no repair to turn fawn (5)

16 Mantrap turns violent (7)

19 I leave chair to become skivvy (4)

20 Without us scriptures are rewritten (8)

22 Sympathy for men? (6, 7)

DOWN

1   I leave burgeon to flame (4)

2   Confusion averts hunger (6)

3   Cartels disrupted are soon in the red (7)

4   Reg leaves Belgrade sharpish (5)

5   Goat as dairy product? (6)

6   Vegetable dye? (3, 5)

11 The deco here reverberated (2-6)

13 Players reassess green stuff (7)

15 Without brown sauce gargoyles make throaty noise (6)

17 Purposeful loss of saucers gives colourful result (6)

18 Igor goes out borrowing with colourful result (5)

21 Pekingese geese take wing, gaily coloured (4)

PUZZLE 350

To fill the grid you must choose the correct words from the following list and then try to make them fit. To make the task more challenging we have given you more words than you actually need.

Answers see page **255**

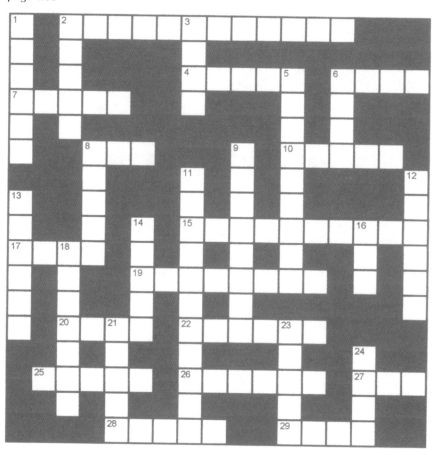

Violet	Cream	Cinnabar	Oatmeal
Royal blue	Ruby	Magnolia	Poppy
Cerise	Ultraviolet	Khaki	Silver
Puce	Green	Aquamarine	Gold
Earth	Russet	Purple	Red	Lilac
Chocolate	Livid	Orange	Navy	Black
Midnight blue	Pink	Rose	Infrared	Jet
Terracotta	Mauve	Scarlet	Sky	Tan
Pea green	Beige	Leaden	Vermilion	Grey
Brown	Indigo	Stone	Denim	Bronze

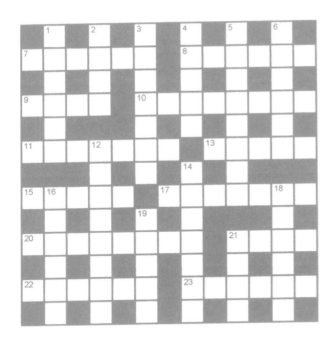

PUZZLE 351

Answers see page **255**

ACROSS

7 The colour! Love it! (6)

8 Robin deserts nonbeliever for football team? (6)

9 Ascended colourfully (4)

10 Campanologist endures small loss for floral tribute (8)

11 Gainsayers deprived of gin conduct analysis (7)

13 Erased from degenerates gives rise to small mammal (5)

15 Troubled heart laid in ground (5)

17 Custard pie ads conceal image (7)

20 Unharnessing gran leads to good weather (8)

21 Ill swelling (4)

22 Save Tory from mediocrity to dominate Florence! (6)

23 Ale leaves Den feeling heavy-headed? (6)

DOWN

1 Lila no longer villainous but rather boozy (6)

2 Car, no longer curable, feels sad (4)

3 Me sm, sm, sma, SMART! (7)

4 Unrepaired gaberdines are a boring colour (5)

5 I watch Eros fret over green project (8)

6 I, Ceres, provide cherry! (6)

12 I sit in cart aesthetically (8)

14 Airborne arsonist? (7)

16 Pasteurizers lacking esprit give us the blues (6)

18 Man deserts submarine, discovers fortune (6)

19 Ashen with rage (5)

21 A bed is uncomfortable place to find trinket (4)

PUZZLE 352

To fill the grid you must choose the correct words from the following list and then try to make them fit. To make the task more challenging we have given you more words than you actually need.

Answers see page **255**

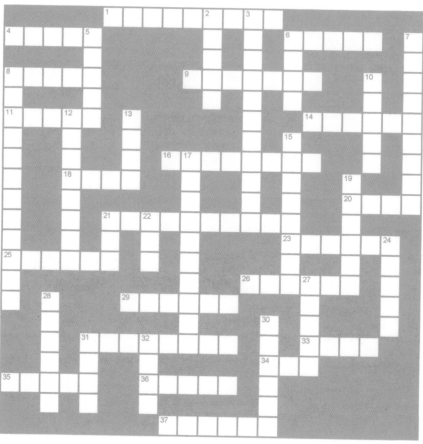

Violet	Cream	Cinnabar	Oatmeal
Royal blue	Ruby	Magnolia	Poppy
Cerise	Ultraviolet	Khaki	Silver
Puce	Green	Aquamarine	Gold
Earth	Russet	Purple	Red	Lilac
Chocolate	Livid	Orange	Navy	Black
Midnight blue	Pink	Rose	Infrared	Jet
Terracotta	Mauve	Scarlet	Sky	Tan
Pea green	Beige	Leaden	Vermilion	Grey
Brown	Indigo	Yellow	Denim	Bronze

PUZZLE 353

Answers see page **255**

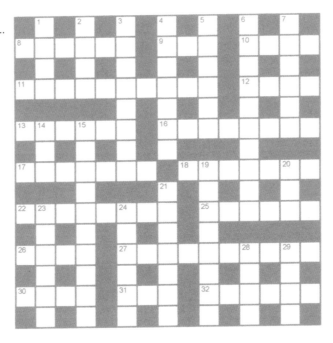

ACROSS

8   'Cos Joe was feeling merry? (6)
9   Shawnee loses chickens in fearful mess (3)
10 I hear you steal computer programs (4)
11 A tad weighed down by mortality? (4, 6)
12 Colour of rouble, or not? (4)
13 Surest way to find the right hue (6)
16 Gran causes colourful mayhem with epee (3, 5)
17 Made glad by a down and out? (3-4)
18 Tabernacles deprived of vegetable become embarrassed? (7)
22 Nun shies from heavenly light? (8)
25 Sharp remark gives rise to grudge? (6)
26 After Hudson left the greyhound's life was a little dull (4)
27 ETA blows up tractor in scorched earth policy (10)
30 Ivan leaves Slovenia, but not in haste we hear (4)
31 Such skin is no longer PC in US (3)
32 Without me menswear provides a response (6)

DOWN

1   Would this girl be as sweet by another name? (4)
2   Lambs played without Mabel and got richer (4)
3   D, thrown out, feels depressed (8)
4   Pendulous problems (4-3)
5   Big girl, sounds like midwife (6)
6   Ant has high hopes of moving this plant? (6, 4)
7   Operating instructions for girl? (6)
14 Rousseau lost his euros and emigrated to the New World (3)
15 Made fashionable by own efforts (4-6)
19 Brain can redden? (8)
20 Jellied slipper? (3)
21 Reg dead? What a disgrace! (7)
23 United Nations staff list, perhaps? (6)
24 Imprison young US doctor (6)
28 Expel Del from loudest (4)
29 Trevelyan loses belly button and gains three! (4)

Colour
Conundrums

Answers

Answer 316
Column 1. All the colours in Col 1 have one syllable, all those in Col 2 have two syllables.

Answer 317
Germany. The colours all have five-letter names.

Answer 318
'This message is hidden.' Take only the letters that have no 'e' in name of the colour.

Answer 319
Taking the colours in alphabetical order: black square, blue heart, brown cube, green crossed circle, orange square, pink sun, purple smiley, red cross, yellow hexagon.

Answer 320
12. Use the number of letters in the name of each colour. Multiply left by centre, subtract right).

Answer 321
The correct order is based on the alphanumeric value of the words. It goes: red (27), blue (40), green (49), pink (50), orange (60), brown (72), purple (88), yellow (92)

Answer 322
2940. Multiply the alphanumeric equivalents of the pairs of colours.

Answer 323
The red rectangle. In all the others the number of sides of the shape is the same as the number of letters in the colour.

Answer 324
The colours all have their basic alphanumeric values. A smiley face multiplies that value by 3, a cube by 2 and a cylinder by 4. Therefore the answer is 108.

Answer 325
The colours all have their basic alphanumeric values. For a smiley face subtract 10, for a cube subtract 5, and for a cylinder subtract 15. Therefore the answer is 73.

Answer 326
'Now is the winter of our discontent.' Letters of the same colour go together.

Answer 327
1. Take the number of letters in the names of the colours. In each column subtract the bottom number from the top.

Answer 328
15. Take the number of letters in the name of each colour and multiply pairs together.

Answer 329
If you use only the red letters you get the message 'Red is the colour'.

Answer 330
The red, black, green and orange letters spell out, 'Wherefore art thou Romeo'.

Answer 331
Where have all the flowers gone.

Answer 332
The colours have their alphanumeric values but the alphabet has been numbered backwards (Z = 1, A = 26). All the shapes are added except for the explosion which is always subtracted.

Answer 333
Answer: Wittgenstein. The letters are all made up of colours with six-letter names (orange, yellow, purple).

Answer 334
Arrows with colours with an E in their name point upwards.

Answer 335
Take only the red numbers. They represent letters of the alphabet numbered backwards (Z = 26, A = 1). The message is: 'This will be hard to decode'.

Answer 336
158. All colours have their alphanumeric value. A smiley face means subtract 20, a heart means subtract 15, a crossed circle means subtract 10,

a star means subtract 5. The value of each row is added and the total placed at the end.

Answer 337

404. The colours have their alphanumeric value (yellow 92, purple 88, orange 60, pink 50, green 49, blue 40). The arrows work as follows: right (x3), left (x2), up (-20), down (-30)

Answer 338

'Another cunning code.' Use only the letters made from colours with six letters in their name (purple, yellow, orange).

Answer 339

If you take only the colours with five letters in their name (green and brown), you get, 'This one is a bit harder'.

Answer 340

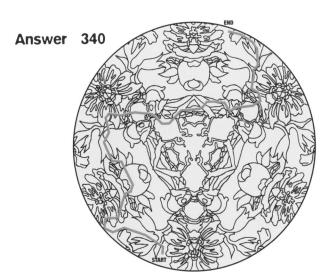

Answer 341

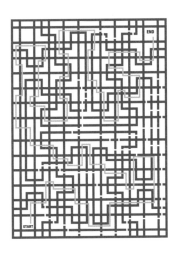

Answer 342

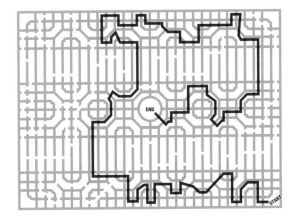

Answer 343

Answer 344

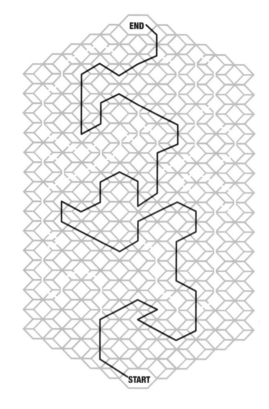

Answer 345

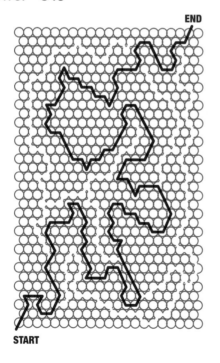

Answer 346

Answer 347

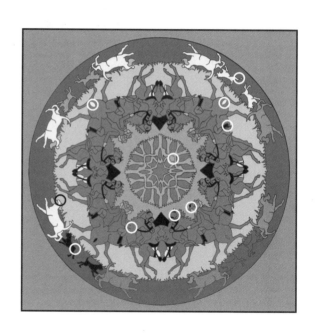

Answer 348

Answer 349

Across: 7 Multi-coloured, 8 Infrared, 9 Toga, 10 Freezer, 12 Green, 14 Beige, 16 Rampant, 19 Char, 20 Rescript, 22 Fellow feeling.
Down: 1 Burn, 2 Starve, 3 Scarlet, 4 Blade, 5 Butter, 6 Pea green, 11 Reechoed, 13 Parsley, 15 Gargle, 17 Purple, 18 Brown, 21 Pink.

Answer 350

Across: 2 Midnight blue, 4 Lilac, 6 Pink, 7 Livid, 8 Sky, 10 Cream, 15 Terracotta, 17 Rose, 19 Pea green, 20 Ruby, 22 Indigo, 25 Denim, 26 Leaden, 27 Red, 28 Earth, 29 Navy.
Down: 1 Violet, 2 Mauve, 3 Gold, 5 Chocolate, 6 Puce, 8 Stone, 9 Infrared, 11 Ultraviolet, 12 Orange, 13 Cerise, 14 Poppy, 16 Tan, 18 Scarlet, 21 Beige, 23 Green, 24 Grey.

Answer 351

Across: 7 Violet, 8 Eleven, 9 Rose, 10 Magnolia, 11 Assayer, 13 Genet, 15 Earth, 17 Picture, 20 Sunshine, 21 Bubo, 22 Medici, 23 Leaden.
Down: 1 Vinous, 2 Blue, 3 Stammer, 4 Beige, 5 Reforest, 6 Cerise, 12 Artistic, 14 Firefly, 16

Azures, 18 Rubies, 19 Livid, 21 Bead.

Answer 352

Across: 1 Royal blue, 4 Lilac, 6 Green, 8 Mauve, 9 Scarlet, 11 Denim, 14 Indigo, 16 Magnolia, 18 Ruby, 20 Rose, 21 Terracotta, 23 Bronze, 25 Leaden, 26 Purple, 29 Cerise, 31 Pea green, 33 Puce, 34 Sky, 35 Brown, 36 Livid, 37 Violet.
Down: 2 Black, 3 Ultraviolet, 5 Cream, 6 Grey, 7 Chocolate, 8 Midnight blue, 10 Beige, 12 Infrared, 13 Navy, 15 Cinnabar, 17 Aquamarine, 19 Orange, 21 Tan, 22 Red, 24 Earth, 27 Poppy, 28 Yellow, 30 Russet, 31 Pink, 32 Gold.

Answer 353

Across: 8 Jocose, 9 Awe, 10 Unix, 11 Dead weight, 12 Blue, 13 Russet, 16 Pea green, 17 Bag-lady, 18 Scarlet, 22 Sunshine, 25 Needle, 26 Grey, 27 Terracotta, 30 Sloe, 31 Red, 32 Answer
Down: 1 Rose, 2 Gold, 3 Dejected, 4 Hang-ups, 5 Bertha, 6 Rubber tree, 7 Misuse, 14 USA, 15 Self-styled, 19 Cinnabar, 20 Eel, 21 Degrade, 23 Unroll, 24 Intern, 28 Oust, 29 Trey.

Many puzzles depend for their solution on so-called alphanumeric values (ie, where letters are used to represent numbers that relate to their position in the alphabet). Below is a table giving these values. Because puzzle-setters are a tricky and vicious breed they sometimes number the alphabet backwards, so we have given you that version as well.

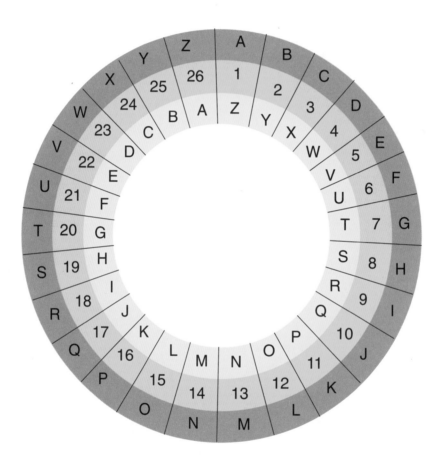

Another useful item is the alphabet formed into a circle. Puzzles that depend on alphabetic order sometimes trick the reader by using this device. Beware!